Supporting Children with
Behaviour Difficulties

Hull Learning Services

 **David Fulton** Publishers

David Fulton Publishers Ltd
The Chiswick Centre, 414 Chiswick High Road, London W4 5TF

www.fultonpublishers.co.uk
www.onestopeducation.co.uk

David Fulton Publishers is a division of Granada Learning Limited, part of ITV plc.

First published 2005, reprinted 2005

Note: The right of the authors to be identified as the authors of this work has been asserted by them in accordance with the Copyright, Designs and Patents Act 1988.

British Library Cataloguing in Publication Data
A catalogue record for this book is available from the British Library.

ISBN 1 84312 228 6

Typeset by FiSH Books, London
Printed and bound in Great Britain

Contents

Foreword

This book was produced in partnership with services based in Kingston Upon Hull, the Hull City Psychological Service and the Educational Service for Physical Disability, and is written by:

Anny Bibby	Educational Psychologist
Mary Davey	SENCO, Ashwell Pupil Referral Unit
Dee Hudson-Vaux	Educational Psychologist
Susan Miller	Senior Educational Psychologist
Elizabeth Morling	ESPD
Carole Stitt	Educational Psychologist

It is one of a series of eleven titles, providing an up-to-date overview of special educational needs for SENCOs, teachers and other professionals and parents. It was produced in response to training and information needs of teachers, support staff and parents in Hull.

The aim of these books is to raise awareness and address many of the issues involved in creating inclusive environments.

For details of other titles and how to order, please go to: www.fultonpublishers.co.uk, or telephone: 0500 618052.

Introduction

From time to time all children can behave in an undesirable way. However, factors such as the age of the child, the context in which the behaviour occurs and the frequency of the behaviour can alter whether a child's behaviour is viewed as a normal part of growing up or as problematic misbehaviour.

Emotional and behavioural difficulties (EBD) is a broad and vague term, which is widely used within education. The Green Paper: *Excellence for All Children: Meeting Special Educational Needs* describes emotional and behavioural difficulties as a term that can be:

> Applied to a broad range of young people – preponderantly boys – with a very wide spectrum of needs, from those with short-term emotional difficulties to those with extremely challenging behaviour or serious psychological difficulties. (DfEE 1997)

Such a definition illustrates the range of difficulties the term 'Emotional and behavioural difficulties' encompasses, and it would appear that it is not possible to provide one single definition of problem behaviour. It is therefore the case that most problem behaviours lie in a continuum between occasional naughtiness and extreme, diagnosable conditions. Furthermore, the meaning and nature of misbehaviour is a dynamic concept which is dependent upon both the context in which it occurs and upon how a particular individual – a pupil, teacher or parent – interprets and perceives the behaviour.

Inclusion issues

Over the last decade, government legislation has emphasised and highlighted the rights of all children, including those with special educational needs. Legislation has also stressed the benefits of inclusive education and indicates that local education authorities should be working towards meeting the needs of the majority of pupils with special educational needs (SEN) in mainstream schools.

For an outline of SEN legislation which impacts on current practice see Appendix 1.

Implications of the Disability Discrimination Act 1995 as amended by the SEN and Disability Act 2001 (SENDA 2001)

Part 1 of the Act:

- strengthens the right of all children to be educated in mainstream schools;

- requires LEAs to arrange for parents and/or children with SEN to be provided with advice on SEN matters, and also a means of settling disputes with schools and LEAs (parent partnership services and mediation/conciliation schemes);

- states that pupils should have access to a broad, balanced and relevant education, which includes the National Curriculum;

- requires schools to tell parents where they are making special educational provision for their child and enables schools to request a statutory assessment of a pupil's needs;

- requires that if a statemented child is at risk of exclusion, an interim review of the statement should take place in order to ensure that all reasonable steps have been taken to avoid it (Code of Practice 9.12); and

- requires the LEA, if placement in a mainstream school would be incompatible with the efficient education of other children, to show that all reasonable steps have been taken to counteract this incompatibility.

The inclusive school

A school that is educationally inclusive is an effective school. Inclusive schools are places where:

- there is an ethos of inclusion that is understood by staff, parents, governors, pupils and the local community;
- achievements of all pupils are valued, recognised and celebrated;
- improving teaching and learning for all pupils is a constant concern for senior managers;
- the wellbeing of all pupils matters and where their attitudes, values and behaviour are constantly challenged and developed;
- staff, pupils and parents treat each other with respect;
- senior managers put into place actions and strategies to ensure that all pupils make better progress.

Schools should offer an inclusive curriculum. Each school should have appropriate systems in place to identify the needs of different groups of pupils and to ensure that its provision meets these needs.

Essentially, therefore, the five principles necessary to develop a more inclusive curriculum require a commitment to:

1. value all learners;
2. set suitable learning challenges for groups and individuals;
3. respond to pupils' diverse learning needs;
4. overcome potential barriers to learning and assessment for individuals and groups of pupils; and
5. make the best use of resources.

The Code of Practice (2001) recognises that:

Children and young people who demonstrate features of emotional and behavioural difficulties, who are withdrawn or isolated, disruptive and disturbing, hyperactive and lack concentration; those with immature social skills; and those presenting challenging behaviours arising from other complex special needs, may require help or counselling for some, or all, of the following:

- Flexible teaching arrangements.
- Help with development of social competence and emotional maturity.
- Help in adjusting to school expectations and routines.
- Help in acquiring the skills of positive interaction with peers and adults.
- Specialised behavioural and cognitive approaches.
- Re-channelling or re-focusing to diminish repetitive and self-injurious behaviours.
- Provision of class and school systems which control or censure difficult behaviours and encourage positive behaviour.
- Provision of a safe and supportive environment.

Section 1

The causes and consequences of behavioural difficulties

Possible consequences of behavioural difficulties

For the majority of children the underlying causes of their emotional and behavioural problems can be attributed to complex interactions between a range of different influences. These include factors to do with the child him/herself, the family and other environmental risk factors; however, the relative importance of each of these factors is highly debated. The flowchart below illustrates the possible consequences of behavioural difficulties.

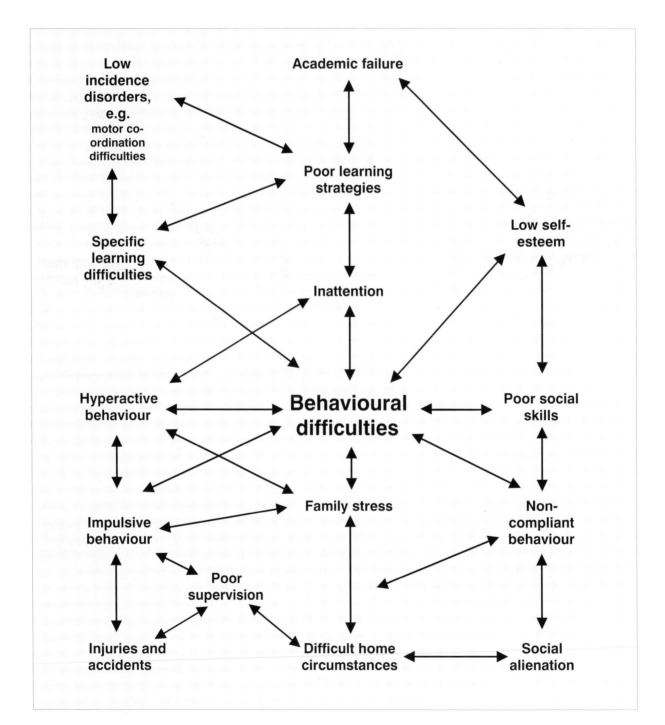

Lowered self-concept/self-esteem

Self-concept may be thought of as like an old-fashioned set of balance scales. On one side are the negative beliefs we have about ourselves; on the other, the positive ones.

These beliefs begin at an early age and are affected by our successes and failures throughout life, and by what we are told about ourselves by our parents, friends, teachers and others. Self-concept is powerful and can influence our performance. For example, a child who has a poor self-concept of him/herself as a learner will not learn as effectively as one with a good self-concept, irrespective of ability levels.

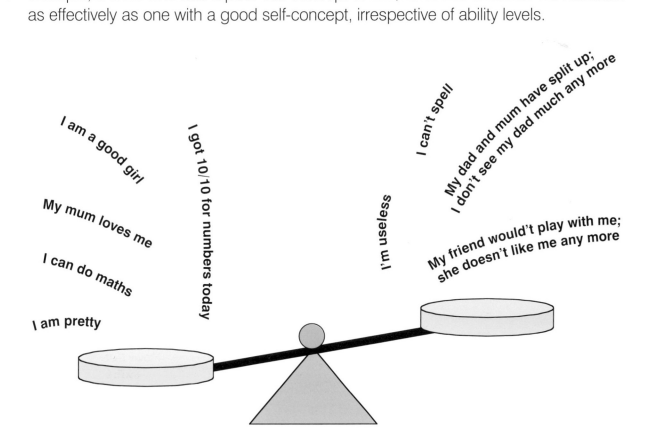

Children do take in and remember things they hear about themselves. This can replay as a kind of self-talk which then guides the expectations and beliefs they hold about themselves and the world. 'Today's talk is tomorrow's thought.' This process will continue unless challenged by different perspectives or experiences.

Strategies to build self-esteem

- Ensure work is achievable and appropriately differentiated.
- Offer frequent reassurance and encouragement.
- Recognise and celebrate effort and perseverance – use rewards.
- Use the magic formula – give at least five positive statements for every criticism.
- Give specific praise (i.e. 'Well done, you ignored Liam when he was…', rather than 'Good boy').
- Focus on strengths and develop talents.
- Affirm positive behaviour frequently. Build success into every day, and reward immediately and generously.
- Intervene as soon as there is a hint of inappropriate behaviour, rather than letting it build.
- Give precise feedback.
- Give responsibility to the pupil.

Difficulties with peer relationships

Pupils who display inappropriate behaviour can easily become isolated from their peer group. Others may avoid them because they do not like the behaviour or because they do not wish to be associated with it. Being unable to develop and sustain rewarding peer relationships will impact on the child's level of self-esteem.

Approaches which aim to build positive peer relationships and friendship skills include:

- an effective anti-bullying policy and anti-bullying procedures;
- developing a positive relationship with the pupil – other pupils will model their behaviour on that of the adults around them.
- making sure the pupil and his/her peers know you like them, even though you do not like their behaviour;
- publicly praising the pupil;
- collaborative groupwork to encourage discussion – pupils learn that they have to co-operate with others in order to complete the task;
- social skills training will help to develop a pupil's communication and interactive skills;
- teaching 'emotional literacy' – there are many games, activities and programmes available to teach skills such as self-awareness, managing feelings and conflict resolution;
- peer mediation and listening services – these can help when friendships have broken down;
- Circle Time – these activities aim to develop a range of skills such as communication and turn-taking, and encourage empathy and understanding of others' difficulties;
- solution-focused approaches such as engaging young people in developing their own goals and action plans;
- cognitive-behavioural approaches which develop children's awareness of why they react as they do, and strategies to overcome these responses; for example, anger management;
- developing support groups and friendship groups. The no-blame approach to bullying and Circle of Friends are specific means of developing support for those with varying difficulties including those displaying bullying behaviour;
- developing buddy systems in school to ensure young people are not left isolated;
- curriculum-based approaches which use drama, art, creative writing and discussion to explore moral dilemmas.

For a list of resources see Appendix 2. Additional resources may also be found in educational catalogues or on the internet. However, the quality of internet sites varies and therefore they should be used with caution.

Relationships and belonging

Dealing with challenging behaviour can be time-consuming, frustrating and stressful. It is therefore vital that within school there is a supportive ethos. Senior management have the responsibility for setting the ethos of the school, and for supporting staff in creating a warm, inclusive and accepting climate.

Developing positive relationships between pupils and staff is also extremely important in eliciting appropriate behaviour from pupils.

Ways to develop good relationships

- Separate the person from the behaviour ('I like you, but not that behaviour').
- Try to see the young person holistically, not just as 'the problem' (talk to them about their interests, hopes and activities).
- Listen before putting your own point of view (it is always easier to listen to someone if you feel you have already been 'heard').
- Speak in a respectful manner (try to avoid unintentional put-downs).
- Manage your own emotions. Avoid shouting or other forms of distancing yourself from the young person (someone who is distressed has enough emotions of their own to cope with without having to cope with yours).
- Try and elicit the desired behaviour through co-operation rather than coercion.
- Find times to provide some individual attention.
- Use humour (sensitively – humour directed at someone who cannot respond is not funny, it is bullying).
- Listen.

The voice of the child

Children need to be included in decision-making because:

- Children have equal rights to participate in discussions that will affect their future.
- Children have the right to express their own points of view even if these contradict those of others.
- School systems, particularly the SEN and exclusionary systems, can often contribute to the creation of a negative identity for the child.
- The UN Convention on the Rights of the Child has legally noted that the voice of the child must be taken into account.
- People need, when making decisions and developing effective strategies, to understand issues from the child's point of view.
- If children are not included they will have no investment in what is taking place.

Strategies for including the child's point of view

- Establish a school council.
- Listen to children and young people and include them in meetings about themselves, e.g. planning meetings and monitoring IEPs.
- Use an advocate if children find meetings intimidating.
- Help children write what they wish to say if this is easier for them.
- Ensure the adults are positive and solution-focused, rather than blaming and personal.
- Use peer advisers or peer groups to promote pupil participation.
- Make sure that children and young people are very clear about, and understand exactly, what the issues are.

Working with parents

- The SEN Code of Practice strongly reinforces the right of parents to be involved in educational decision-making concerning their child.
- Be aware of the differences in power between the professionals and parents.
- Parents should not be made to feel disempowered, sidelined or criticised as ineffective by the school.
- Criticism of their children often arouses powerful feelings of guilt, shame and embarrassment in parents, and they might oppose or reject the school's views because of these feelings.
- Parents may have had negative experiences of school themselves and this can lead to a variety of responses, including taking their child's side against the school.
- Parents may have struggled to get recognition of a diagnosis and so continue to be sensitive to professional opinions.
- Do not make assumptions and attributions based on the race, culture or gender of children and their families.
- Be aware that misunderstandings happen around different attitudes, beliefs, value systems and expectations.

When working with families:

- Be positive. Think, 'Everyone is doing their best, given their circumstances and the information available'.
- Be proactive. Make sure you work with parents when things are going well. Meet regularly to discuss ongoing progress.
- Listen to parents: they have a different, alternative and valid perspective.
- Work collaboratively by sharing information and expertise.
- Become active partners with parents and professionals ('sing from the same hymn-sheet').
- Make meetings friendly and supportive.
- Build trust and mutual respect by using informal situations to encourage dialogue. Look for solutions via other possibilities.

When parents are 'resistant' or 'won't engage'

Reasons why parents do not engage can be complex. They could be because:

- They do not feel they are being listened to.
- They do not feel they are being treated with respect.

- They are asked to do something of which they are not capable.
- They do not engage with the educational culture.

Follow the ideas suggested when working with families. If there are still difficulties:

- Make sure good records are kept of discussions, agreements and actions taken.
- Make sure there are clear, consistent boundaries and consequences.
- Monitor progress carefully.
- Follow school procedures carefully, including those relating to discipline.
- Liaise with other agencies and services including Education Welfare and Social Services.

The Pastoral Support Plan (PSP)

Pastoral Support Plans (PSPs) were introduced in the governmental guidance *Circular 10/99, Social Inclusion: Pupil Support as a means of supporting pupils who are at significant risk of permanent exclusion.*

A PSP is intended for the small minority of pupils who display significant behavioural and/or emotional difficulties. Pupils who are likely to require a PSP include:

- pupils who have had several fixed-term exclusions and who are at risk of permanent exclusion;
- pupils who are re-integrating back into school following long-term absence;
- pupils integrating into a new school following a permanent exclusion from their previous school;
- pupils who have profound emotional and/or behavioural difficulties following a traumatic life event, e.g. change in family circumstances following separation of parents, a death in the family or being taken into care.

A PSP does not replace the strategies and systems already in place to support pupils' special educational needs. Rather a PSP is a multi-agency intervention that brings together the pupil, parents/carers, school, LEA and other appropriate agencies so that they can work collaboratively to discuss concerns and take positive steps to help address a pupil's behavioural difficulties. When a school sets up a PSP it must inform the LEA. LEAs have a responsibility to help schools with pupils who have PSPs. This help might include:

- attending the PSP and offering advice and support;
- additional financial support;
- supporting the pupil through joint registration at their present school and a Pupil Referral Unit (PRU);
- supporting the pupil in a managed move to another school.

The agreed plan is developed within an inter-agency meeting, held usually within school, and is monitored regularly through further meetings. The needs of the pupil are considered, and the ways that these may be addressed through appropriate support, e.g. the social worker may look for a stable, long-term placement; the school may provide opportunities for the pupil to talk to a mentor, or arrange a 'time out' system for when the pupil feels he/she is losing control. The youth worker may be able to offer out-of-school, age-appropriate activities. As part of this, the pupil will collaborate on setting his/her own targets. Targets are reviewed and modified, if necessary fortnightly. The optimum length of time for a plan to run is stated to be sixteen weeks.

When running a PSP, bear in mind the following points:

- Be positive about change; look at solutions rather than problems.
- Include the pupil's views; depending on age, have the pupil present at the meeting. For younger pupils, talk to them beforehand about their wishes and feelings.
- The potential of the PSP increases where other agencies are involved, and where changes in systems – in school or at home – are made a reality.
- Use the PSP to collate and exchange information, and as a way to look at the whole picture.
- Be clear about boundaries and roles; use subsequent meetings to ensure agreements have been kept, by adults as well as by the pupil.
- Work towards improving outcomes for the pupil as well as for the school.
- View the PSP as a means of inclusion, not a tick-box *en route* to exclusion.
- Expect that it will not be an instant remedy; give it time to work. Use the PSP to support all participants when there are 'blips'.
- For a pupil with a Statement, an interim Annual Review may be called.

Try to avoid:
- focusing on changing the pupil rather than the systems around him/her;
- making the PSP merely a 'paper exercise'.

There is no set format for recording a PSP, and it is down to individual schools to develop recording systems that work for them. An effective PSP may include the following:

- pupil details, e.g. name, DOB, gender, year group, family circumstances;
- a pupil's individual strengths/interests – these should include the pupil's interests and achievements both in and out of school;
- details of a pupil's learning style, academic strengths and learning difficulties;
- details and outcomes of previous interventions;
- clear identification of the nature of the pupil's current behavioural difficulties, e.g. frequency, duration, triggers, consequences, impact/reaction of peers/staff;
- details of the planned intervention – these should identify SMART targets, provision/resources, staff to be involved, systems of liaising between different parties, how and when the intervention will be evaluated, rewards and sanctions.

For an example of a Pastoral Support Plan and a blank proforma, see Appendix 3.

Section 2

Whole-school strategies/ approaches to behavioural difficulties

Whole-school thinking

- A whole-school focus is the most effective way of minimising or preventing the occurrence of behavioural problems.

- School is a complex social community and has a role in the development and/or prevention of behaviour, and therefore should develop whole-school behaviour/discipline policies with an emphasis on positive strategies to promote good behaviour.

- Policies should unite staff towards a common ethos in which all staff feel supported when faced with difficulties.

- All organisations have inherent points of conflict and tension. Children with behavioural difficulties often magnify these stresses and tensions.

- Head teachers and senior managers are responsible for creating the conditions for establishing and maintaining discipline policies in schools.

- Curriculum content and how it is delivered are important influences on pupil's behaviour.

- Involving parents, pupils, ancillary staff and governors develops and maintains good behaviour and positive relationships in and around school.

- A small minority of incidents may require the pupil to be physically restrained. Schools should have a physical intervention policy and all staff should be very clear about the set procedures involved. For additional information, legal guidelines and advice on writing a physical intervention policy see Appendix 4.

Whole-school issues

What in the school situation is helping to maintain the behaviour?	The institution itself can support undesirable behaviour.
What are people focusing on – problems or solutions?	Focusing on solutions is more constructive, productive and is more likely to bring about change.
Do you have a whole-school discipline/behaviour policy and is it a paper exercise or is it a working document?	Are the words on paper translated into action?
Is everyone in the school clear about the route from behavioural difficulties to desirable outcome?	Would a supply teacher coming into the school easily understand the system?
Is every member of staff helping the senior management team to lead effectively?	Everyone has a responsibility to work towards positive discipline; enthusiasm, commitment and communication are all necessary ingredients.
Do you talk as a staff team about long-term solutions as well as short-term responses?	Creative thinking about how to prevent similar difficulties arising in the future is helpful.
Do all staff have clear common goals regarding behaviour?	Is there a consistent approach by all staff throughout the school?
Do all members of staff feel well supported?	Do you problem-solve jointly as a staff and support each other under stress?
What are the relationships like between pupils, staff, support staff, parents, governors and the community?	Hostility will be damaging to the school's positive interactions.
Do you have access to training, receive ongoing support and have time to plan, review and reflect on behaviour programmes?	An effective team ensures colleagues are appropriately skilled and can translate this into their everyday work.

Effective learning environments

Pupils with behavioural difficulties require even greater structure and organisation than their average peers.

Consider the following:

- physical arrangement of the classroom;
- general classroom organisation;
- discipline policy;
- lesson content and organisation;
- how instructions and directions are given;
- differentiation of curriculum;
- rewards and sanctions.

Physical arrangement of the classroom

- Try to integrate individuals rather than isolating them.
- Be aware of potential distractions within and around the classroom. Attempt to minimise them.
- Adapt the classroom layout to meet both curriculum demands and the needs of pupils.
- Ensure all materials are easily accessible and clearly labelled.
- Reduce clutter.
- Consider using different combinations of rows for individual desks and a variety of groupings of tables.
- Rows may be beneficial for independent work.
- To aid discussion, arrange the tables in a horseshoe shape.

Effective teaching strategies

- Position the pupil close to the teacher (ensuring that this is seen as a privilege rather than a punishment). This will enable:
  - easy and discreet observation;
  - reinforcement of instructions;
  - giving of immediate praise and feedback.

  Alternatively, position the pupil at the front of the class, facing forward to reduce distractions.

- Provide good role models, preferably pupils perceived by their peers as having good 'street cred'.

- Encourage peer tutoring and co-operative/collaborative learning.

- Provide an independent work area, as free as possible from distractions. Avoid:
    - noisy heating appliances;
    - high-traffic areas;
    - doors or windows;
    - stimulating displays;
    - flickering/bright lights;
    - strong sunlight.

Allow this to be used by any pupil for greater concentration and to ensure that the pupil with behavioural difficulties does not feel ostracised.

- Provide structure for pupils with behavioural difficulties. Assist them with organising their work. Try providing clearly marked trays for unfinished and completed work.

- Pupils who have behavioural difficulties may also have difficulties holding and manipulating information in their working memory. These difficulties will clearly impact on their behaviour, motivation and concentration, and need to be acknowledged and catered for.

- Unambiguous behavioural expectations are a crucial element of effective communication between teachers and their pupils.

- Structure and consistent routines are essential to bring about more desirable behavioural responses from all pupils, not only those who experience behavioural difficulties.

- When changes in routine are unavoidable, inform pupils in advance of future changes. When this is not possible, an appropriate explanation should be given and any new arrangements clearly explained.

- All pupils work more effectively when they understand what is expected of them and the purpose of a lesson. Outline the content and the structure of the school day, and the learning objectives and format of each lesson.

Effective teaching strategies

- At the beginning of a new academic year, daily/weekly routines need to be explained and practised and behavioural expectations established. This is particularly important for potentially problematic times such as the beginnings and endings of lessons and for transition times when a large number of pupils are involved.

- For some pupils, verbal reminders of routines and/or lesson content will need to be visually reinforced, e.g. by displaying a weekly timetable prominently in the classroom or for individual pupils via a visual timetable.

- Time checks throughout a lesson enable pupils to monitor their own rate of progress on a task and provide them with an indication of how much longer they have left.

- A kitchen timer or an alarm clock is a useful visual tool. Such devices may be used to indicate, visually, the length of time a teacher expects the class to work independently while concentrating on a specific group within the class. Pupils should be praised for demonstrating the desired behaviour, and the length of time can be increased gradually as the class develops successfully.

Additional teaching strategies for older pupils

- Remind pupils of the routines expected at the beginnings, during the transitions and at the ends of lessons.

- Reinforce the routine, lesson by lesson.

- Specify clearly which activities are strictly 'in-seat' and when free movement is permitted.

- Plan ahead and give advance warning of a forthcoming change of activity or the end of the current lesson.

- Allow adequate time for 'finishing off' and for clearing away equipment.

- Establish clear routines for communicating with parents, e.g. via a pupil planner, and use these regularly.

Behavioural management

- A consistent system of rewards and sanctions is likely to be a key element of any classroom management strategy.
- Consider a range of strategies to deal with problem behaviour, as some strategies will work better with certain pupils than others and some will work one day and not the next.
- Target only one or two aspects of behaviour at a time. Make clear what is not acceptable and what is desired. Pupils respond most positively when there are clear expectations.
- The behavioural management of an individual pupil is the responsibility of all members of staff, not just the class teacher.
- A united and uniform application of rules and sanctions is vital, and should follow the guidelines and strategies as outlined in the school's behaviour policy.

Effective teaching strategies

- All rules and sanctions need to be clear and concise. Examples of both keeping and breaking the rules should be modelled regularly and reinforced, not just highlighted at times of crisis.
- Behavioural targets need to be both achievable and measurable.
- Desirable classroom behaviours need to be frequently reinforced.
- Praise the specific behaviour, e.g. 'I liked the way you put your hand up when you knew the answers', rather than 'good boy' or 'well done'.
- Remind a pupil of the expected behaviour, rather than pointing out their negative actions, e.g. instead of 'Stop shouting out the answers', say 'Put up your hand if you know the answer'.
- Praise good behaviour and work frequently to ensure motivation and task appliance.
- Concrete rewards are usually more successful as these offer a tangible reminder to the pupil of how well he/she is doing.
- Rewards, such as a star chart or tokens that can be exchanged at a later time for a favourite activity or treat, are effective.
- Response–cost programmes can also be very effective. Reward good behaviour and work with tokens or marbles in a jar. Remove them for undesirable behaviour.
- Address pupils in a calm and reasonable manner.
- Deal with undesirable behaviour from close proximity rather than shouting from across the room, to avoid disrupting the rest of the class.
- Avoid strategies that allow the pupil to gain an audience.

Additional teaching strategies for older pupils

- Mutually agree with the pupils a limited number of clear and achievable classroom rules. Ensure that all the pupils understand them.
- Displaying these rules in the classroom acts as a useful visual reminder.
- Use SMART targets: **S**pecific, **M**easurable, **A**chievable, **R**ealistic, **T**ime-limited.

Lesson organisation

- Good teaching practice for all pupils is closely linked to the skills and qualities required to work effectively with pupils who experience behavioural difficulties.
- Through thorough planning and preparation it is possible to anticipate and minimise many potential difficulties.

Effective teaching strategies

- Ensure that all relevant teaching materials and equipment are well organised and easily accessible.
- At the start of a lesson provide the whole class with an overview of the format the lesson will take.
- Emphasise the learning objectives so that the class knows in advance what will be expected of it.
- Support working memory with external prompts:
  - visual reminders of the work;
  - written reminders for whole-class use;
  - individual written schedules;
  - instructional posters;
  - displays of key words and facts.
- Use a multi-sensory format when delivering lessons.
- Vary the pace of the lesson.
- Include a range of activities, including those that require a higher degree of sustained concentration and effort, and those which involve more physical responses.
- Break activities down into manageable stages so that only one piece of information needs to be processed at a time. When one stage has been completed successfully, the next stage can then be presented.
- During the course of a lesson allow sufficient time for a plenary when the content of the lesson and the learning objectives can be reviewed and reinforced.

Additional teaching strategies for older pupils

- Prepare in advance to ensure a prompt, purposeful start to the lesson, with resources available.
- Set a variety of tasks and activities that provide sufficient differentiation and challenge.
- Vary the pace of the lesson, tone of your voice and method of delivery. When possible, include some 'active' tasks as well as 'in-seat' ones.

- Use multi-sensory approaches to teaching and learning.
- Allow adequate time for each part of a lesson.
- Set SMART, achievable targets.
- When a pupil completes a task, praise his/her efforts (be it privately or in front of the whole class) and ensure that there are additional activities available for the pupils to progress towards.
- Encourage pupils to both visualise and verbalise information or concepts they are being taught.
- During lessons that employ a co-operative learning approach, make sure that every pupil has been assigned a specific role.
- At the end of a lesson, recap not just the learning points but also highlight any other achievements, e.g. pupils who have demonstrated effective listening, supported their peers.

Giving instructions

- Maintain appropriate eye contact during verbal instruction.
- Make directions as clear and concise as possible and be consistent with daily instructions.
- Simplify complex directions and try to avoid multiple commands.
- Make sure that all the pupils understand the instructions before they begin the task.
- Help the pupils feel comfortable when seeking additional assistance or clarification.
- Repeat instructions in a calm and positive manner when required.
- Gradually reduce the amount of assistance, but pupils with behavioural difficulties may need more help for a longer period of time than the average pupil.
- When completing a homework diary, make sure each pupil writes down all assignments correctly. If a pupil is not capable of this, a prepared slip of paper could be pasted into the book.

School work

- Give out only one task at a time.

- Monitor frequently and try to maintain a supportive attitude.

- Differentiate and modify assignments as needed. Consult with the SENCO to determine the specific strengths and weaknesses of each pupil for an IEP.

- In more formal testing situations, ensure that you are testing knowledge and not attention span.

- Some pupils may require additional time or may benefit from undertaking the test in several short bursts.

- Bear in mind that pupils with behavioural difficulties can easily become frustrated. Stress, pressure and fatigue can break down their self-control and lead to poor behaviour.

Rewards and sanctions

- Reward more than you punish, in order to build self-esteem.
- Praise immediately any and all good behaviour and performance.
- Change rewards if they are not effective in motivating behavioural change.
- Find ways to encourage the pupil.
- Teach the pupil to reward him/herself. Encourage positive self-talk (e.g. 'You did very well remaining in your seat today. How do you feel about that?').
- Some children prefer private rather than public praise (there is a need to know the child).
- Remain calm and avoid debating or arguing with the pupil.
- Have pre-established consequences for misbehaviour.
- Administer consequences immediately, and monitor proper behaviour frequently.
- Enforce classroom rules consistently.
- Make sure the discipline fits the crime, without being over-harsh.
- Avoid ridicule and criticism; remember that pupils with behavioural difficulties have difficulty staying in control.

See Appendix 5 for examples of rewards and sanctions and positive behaviour certificates.

Play/breaktimes and lunchtimes

Many pupils find it difficult to maintain appropriate behaviour during unstructured times, e.g. at lunch and breaktime. For these pupils it is necessary to provide alternatives to enable them to have less troublesome breaks, which consequently allow them to return to lessons in a calm manner.

Dinner ladies may require training in appropriate ways to deal with pupils. Schemes such as Lunchbox may support this. Other ideas may come from *Guidelines for Primary Midday Supervisory Assistants* and *Create Happier Lunchtimes*. There are ideas for activities in Appendix 6.

Suggestions to support primary pupils

- Some pupils may need the lunchtime session to be broken down into smaller components, with appropriate behaviour rewarded.
- Put some structure into lunchtime sessions, e.g. 15 minutes helping a teacher to do a job, a short time to play football, time for lunch, followed by structured play.
- Provide activities such as lunchtime clubs and structured groups to play table-top games. This minimises problematic incidents.
- Structured outdoor games organised by dinner supervisors or support assistants should help to improve playground behaviour.
- Extra support may be required for those pupils who need help to learn the rules and be guided in their behaviour.
- Peer monitoring or 'buddy' systems for younger pupils may help to guide pupils to purposeful activities in the playground.

Some of the above may be written into a behavioural IEP if lunchtimes pose problems for a pupil.

Suggestions to support secondary pupils

- Some pupils may require a space to retreat to at lunchtime where they can be quiet or seek out the company of a support assistant.
- Some pupils may benefit from an area where there are fewer pupils around but which gives opportunities for card games and so on to take place, supervised by older pupils or learning mentors who could support and extend social skills.
- The availability of lunchtime clubs (e.g. computer clubs) would provide areas away from the main body of pupils, but would, again, need some support to access the activities successfully.

Early Years

Adults working with young children need to create an environment of support, encouragement and acceptance. Children can be helped to change their behaviour; it is a skill to be acquired, just like other skills in other areas of the curriculum and life.

Perceived difficulties	Strategies
Children who are reluctant to do as adults request	• Children's co-operation needs to be given while allowing them to develop a sense of independence. • Develop simple group rules to which the children contribute. • Treat the child in a calm manner.
Noisy children in a larger group	• Allow opportunities for children to explore with their voices, musical instruments and so on. • Create quiet areas. • Have areas with sound absorbing materials.

Tantrums	• Provide outlets for violent emotions:
	  – Clay to bang
	  – Balls to kick
	  – Music to listen to
	  – Books and stories to be talked about.
	• Avoid children using tantrums to manipulate adults by giving the attention they want in more acceptable ways.

Inability to play with others	• Teach them how to play and get on with other children. • Set up adult-supported paired/small-group opportunities. • Use a small steps approach to develop social and friendship skills. • Develop Circle Time activities.
Biting	• Biting can happen when the child is under pressure, is angry, excited, feeling affectionate or can not express him/herself.

Perceived difficulties	Strategies

	• Observe to identify the triggers/situation when the child is more likely to bite. Try to avoid these situations. If this is not possible, intervene and redirect the child.
	• If a child does not understand that biting is unacceptable and does not comprehend lengthy explanations about why biting is wrong,
	  – Interrupt the biting with a sharp 'No!'
	  – Follow with a sharp phrase 'Biting hurts, we never bite people'
	  – Focus attention on the injured party rather than on the biter, who may take even negative attention as reinforcement for doing it again
	  – Turn away and play with someone else
	  – Praise the child for not biting – especially when they are in situations in which they used to bite or when they are with particular children whom they have previously bitten.

Children with disabilities or learning difficulties can show behaviour which is more characteristic of much younger children	• Adapt the level of support, language and expectations in response to the child's difficulties. • Provide developmentally appropriate equipment and activities.
Children with co-ordination difficulties	• Observe in different areas to determine whether it is an overall problem requiring intervention. • Encourage children to join in gross motor activities (supervision may be needed if the child lacks a sense of danger). • Give support and encouragement to take part in activities, which will help to develop fine motor skills.

Perceived difficulties	Strategies
Children who are engrossed in play can sometimes unwittingly disrupt others	• Draw the child's attention to this and talk to him/her about it. • Consider the room and space required for various activities.
Children who deliberately disrespect property	• This may indicate unhappiness and a lack of commitment or belonging to the setting. • Observe the child. • Speak to the parents to gain clues as to why the child behaves in this way and to discuss the most appropriate way forward.
Short attention/concentration span	• Select shorter stories and books which have very visual features, e.g. pop-up pictures. • Use objects which children can hold, e.g. from Story Sacks. • Turning the pages of the book may help to maintain attention. • Each child holds an object from a story, e.g. the foods from *The Hungry Caterpillar*, and has to listen for the name of his/her object to be read out and place it in an appropriate place. • Short tasks, which are built up in length as the child's concentration improves. • Encouragement to sit to complete a task rather than standing. • 'Engineering' to finish a task, e.g. the adult puts in some jigsaw pieces and the child puts in the last one, so that the child perceives that he/she has finished it. • Praise for completing a task.
Hitting	• Observe. • Respond in a similar way to the response to biting.
Verbal abuse	• Observe and discuss the issues with parents. • Use stories that educate children on issues like racism or sexism, e.g. *Skin I'm In* by Pat Thomas.

Perceived difficulties	Strategies
Communication difficulties	• Use visual timetables made with photographs to show what is to happen during a session. • Use short, simple sentences accompanied by gestures.
Attention-seeking	• Adult attention is vital for children's physical and emotional well-being. Some children constantly seek adult attention. Observe and discuss the possible reasons with parents. • These children still require praise and attention but for positive reasons.
Quiet/withdrawn children	• These children can easily be overlooked because it does not usually rate as a problem. Observation will help to decide if the quietness is caused by fear, distress or a lack of self-esteem. • Discuss with home/carers to establish if the behaviour is across all settings or not. • Unusually quiet children or passive children require just as much thought and input as the child who is grossly attention-seeking.

See Appendix 5 for examples of rewards and sanctions in the early years.

Section 3

Strategies for support staff

Effective support in the classroom

- Be prepared for the lesson and arrive on time to guide pupils to their seats.
- Hand out equipment and books immediately to avoid wasting time.
- Lend pens, pencils and other items (have spare equipment) to avoid time-wasting.
- Encourage pupils to start tasks immediately.
- Reinforce teacher's instructions.
- Interpret, reinforce and repeat instructions if necessary.
- Encourage pupils to stay on task by giving plentiful praise and rewards.
- Encourage and redirect pupils back to the task in hand if their attention wanders.
- Reinforce good behaviour positively by using plenty of smiles and nods.
- Use humour, never sarcasm, and keep the tone of your voice and comments positive.
- Acknowledge even the smallest achievement made by a pupil.
- Avoid making negative comparisons with brothers and sisters and/or others in the classroom.

Working in the classroom

- Observation skills are very important – use your ears and eyes constantly.
- Look at the group at regular intervals to check behaviour (you will need to check more in a less structured time when pupils have less guidance).
- Check the behaviour of the child when working/playing alone.
- Observe the behaviour of pupils working/playing in a group.
- Observe difficulties between members of, and within, the group.
- Try to look at why a pupil is behaving in a particular way rather than simply reacting to an incident.
- Looking at what has contributed to a disturbance may help to stop it happening again.
- Try to step in quickly in a quiet, calm way if behaviour starts to go badly.
- Anticipate where things may go wrong and try to move the pupil on to another activity.
- Move the interactions between the adult and the pupil forward carefully.
- Try to create a rhythm or a particular pace which feels comfortable for all (the pupil, the group and you).
- Learn to recognise when to step in and speak to a pupil and when to leave it to the teacher. Sometimes stepping in will disturb the lesson.
- Make sure pupils are treated in the same way. Avoid favouring the pupil you work with, or being harder on him/her than others in the class.
- Try to respond in the same way each time and in the way the pupil would expect.

Using visual cues

Visual cues are visual hints for pupils who become confused by, or who do not understand, verbal instructions. These can take the form of timetables, cue cards, desk sequences, reminders on the blackboard of work to be done or ticks to show good behaviour.

- The expected task can be given in a visual way as well as a verbal one. For example:

    1. Collect science book.
    2. Open at page 32.
    3. Read pages 32 and 33.
    4. Answer questions 1, 2, 3.
    5. Put your hand up when you have finished.

- Lists or pictures on the board or on charts can show pupils how to get on with their work.

- Showing that behaviour is right or wrong can be done non-verbally. For example:
    - Smiling, frowning, giving a nod, thumbs up; shaking the head draws less attention to the pupil than verbal comments.
    - Eye gaze (eye contact for a long time) can show the pupil that he/she should change his/her behaviour.
    - Standing next to the pupil can be used to indicate that you have noticed the pupil.
    - Visual cue cards and other visual aids may be used for pupils who need more than just gestures. These may be designed and made by the pupil.

Support staff: guidelines for working with pupils

Try to avoid...

Do...

Do...	Try to avoid...
Help the child see his/her mistake and how to overcome it.	asking the pupil 'Why did you do that?' when they don't know themselves. This may cause children to lie.
Tell the pupil what you would like him/her to do.	telling the pupil what you **don't** want him to do.
Look for answers to the pupil's unwanted behaviour.	concentrating on the pupil's crimes or problems all the time.
Sidestep confrontations whenever possible.	getting into an argument with the pupil.
Attempt to offer choices.	insisting on only one type of work from the pupil.
Consider the pupil's learning environment.	focusing solely on trying to change the pupil.
Provide a clear, predictable learning environment.	cluttered areas.
Make it clear that you like and respect the pupil even when you don't like his/her behaviour.	socially rejecting the pupil.
Ensure instructions are at the appropriate level and goals are achievable.	making unrealistic demands on the pupil.

Do...	Try to avoid...
Give the pupil opportunities to develop choice-making skills.	making all the decisions for the pupil.
Encourage independent behaviour and work.	encouraging dependence on support staff.
Work with other pupils while keeping an eye on the pupil you are assigned to.	sitting next to the pupil at all times.
Encourage interaction with peers or allow the pupil to be solitary, to follow his/her own interests.	offering too close an oversight during breaks and lunchtimes.
Encourage the pupil to carry things out independently, e.g. ensuring drawers are clearly labelled.	collecting equipment for the pupil or putting it away.
Ensure work is at an appropriate level and can be carried out with minimal support (note any support given).	completing a task for a pupil.
Give short instructions at the pupil's level of development, with visual prompts.	using language inappropriate for the pupil.
Make sure that the pupil knows what to do. Expect a task to be completed.	making unnecessary allowances for the pupil.
Observe the pupil: determine reasons for behaviour and consider if changes can be made.	tolerating undesirable behaviour.

Section 4

Strategies to address specific behavioural issues

How well do you know this pupil?

Observing a pupil's behaviour

Carrying out a classroom observation is one way of developing a greater understanding of a pupil's behavioural strengths and difficulties. Observation can be used as a way of answering specific questions such as:

- how frequently a pupil behaves in a certain way/manner;
- how a pupil is able/unable to cope with different types of classroom organisation/activities;
- how the pupil responds to a particular teaching style;
- whether or not the classroom tasks are appropriate in terms of the pupil's ability, cultural background and so on.

A one-off observation only provides a snapshot of how a pupil behaved in that particular lesson, on that particular day, at that particular time, for that particular teacher, and is insufficient by itself to form a true picture of a pupil's 'typical' behaviour. Ideally the pupil should be observed over several lessons, until the observer is satisfied that all aspects of the pupil's behaviour – both positive and negative – have been observed.

What should be observed?

Many pupils display more than one type of challenging behaviour. It is not realistic to expect to be able to address and change all behavioural difficulties in one go, so priorities need to be established.

It is vital that the behaviours to be observed are identified and described in observable terms. For example, rather than non-compliant behaviour it would be clearer to describe the number of times the targeted pupil refuses to follow the teacher's instructions/directions.

There are many aspects of a pupil's behaviour that you may want to study. For example:

- How does the pupil respond to whole-class or individual instructions?
- What are the pupil's work habits?
- Can the pupil work independently?
- How much work does the pupil produce compared to others of the same ability within the class?
- Concentration span.

- The type and duration of restless/inattentive behaviour.
- How much teacher attention the pupil demands/secures.
- How much time a pupil spends on or off task.
- How much time the pupil spends on/out of his/her seat.
- The extent/manner to which the pupil interacts with his/her peers.
- To what extent do his/her peers influence the pupil?

How should the observations be done?

Once the target behaviour/behaviours have been agreed upon, the next step is to select a method of recording the observations. Using prepared schedules, such as those given as examples within this book, can be useful, although many teachers seem to prefer creating their own. Observation sheets can take a number of different formats:

Narrative observation

This provides a running commentary on how a pupil behaves. It can take the form of a diary that spans a particular length of time, e.g. a day or a week, or it could be a single-lesson recording that tracks a pupil's behaviour from the beginning through to the end of a lesson. It provides an overview of the range of behaviours – both positive and negative – that the pupil displays.

Time-sampling observation

This is useful when behaviours are easily identified and occur frequently. It is an effective way of highlighting difficulties which may arise within particular parts of a lesson. However, this type of observation merely records the observable behaviour and can omit influencing factors such as the context in which the behaviour occurs, peer influence, task demands and so on. A useful modification to this type of observation is to randomly select another pupil within the class to act as a control.

Event sampling

This approach can help you learn more about the frequency, duration and severity of the targeted behaviour. Recording can be as simple as using a straightforward frequency count, a stopwatch and a rating scale that rates the behaviour from 0 (not evident) to 10 (extreme). Alternatively, this method may also be used to record and analyse one particular incident, or infrequent events. Due consideration should be given to the influencing factors such as the context in which the behaviour occurred, events that preceded the incident (antecedents), the behaviour itself and the consequences that have resulted from the incident. This approach is called the ABC analysis of behaviour.

Tracking

This ongoing form of observation provides a less in-depth, but longitudinal, picture of how a pupil behaves over a longer period of time in a variety of contexts with different adults. This is particularly useful for older pupils who are taught by several different members of staff, and can highlight when a pupil has particular difficulties at certain times of the school day, week, or in particular curriculum areas.

This is by no means a fully comprehensive list of all the different types of observation that can be carried out. All of the above formats have advantages and disadvantages. Be aware of observer bias and try to see things from the pupil's perspective – only record what you actually see – not your own personal inferences. The most important thing is that the approach used works for the observer and results in greater understanding of the difficulties the targeted pupil faces.

Analysing the information gathered

Whatever type of observation is selected, when analysing the resulting information the following considerations must be borne in mind:

- How will the information obtained from the observation be used to plan the ways forward for the pupil's learning and behaviour?
- What are the main causes for concern highlighted by the observation?
- Are the targeted behaviour/behaviours evident in all lessons or are they limited to specific times and places?
- For whom does the behaviour pose a problem – the pupil, the teacher or the pupil's peers?
- Does the highlighted behaviour/behaviours interfere with the pupil's learning or the learning of others? If so, how?
- Does the behaviour put either the pupil or his/her peers/adults at risk? If so, how?
- How do the pupil's peers/adults generally respond to the behaviours causing concern?
- What form will an effective intervention strategy take? How long should this intervention last? How, and by whom, will it be evaluated?

Observations also impart a great deal of information regarding the teaching style, strengths and weakness of the pupil's class/subject teacher, and, if handled sensitively, can be a valuable exercise to share the findings of an observation with the teacher concerned.

See Appendix 7 for examples of observation schedules.

Inattention

Characteristics

- Inability to sustain attention, particularly for repetitive, structured and less enjoyable tasks.
- Problems with concentration – is easily distracted.
- Often appears not to be listening, and has difficulty following and remembering instructions.
- Disorganised; makes careless mistakes.
- Forgetful, e.g. forgets to bring PE kit/homework; loses things.
- Puts off starting tasks and often fails to finish set work.
- Daydreams and can seem oblivious to what is going on.

Effective teaching strategies

- Provide immediate and frequent feedback on behaviour and redirection back to task. The pupil should be actively involved in the setting of targets that focus on attention and task completion.
- Seat pupil near positive role models who will not allow themselves to be distracted.
- Include a variety of activities during each lesson. Introducing a change in activities and position may enable the pupil to return to the original task with renewed focus.
- Seating the pupil at the front of the class and directing frequent questions to him/her will help attention to the lesson.
- Work out a non-verbal signal with the pupil, e.g. a gentle pat on the shoulder or a private signal for times when he/she is not attending and when a verbal reminder would be inappropriate.
- Give out work one activity at a time and adapt coursework to the pupil's attention span, breaking longer pieces of work into smaller parts.

Attention-seeking behaviour

Characteristics

- Emotionally immature.
- Over-friendly, overly helpful.
- Sycophantic; uses flattery to keep a person in authority on side.
- Makes excuses for everything.
- Shows a lot of indignation, especially when challenged.
- Feigns innocence when held accountable, usually by bursting into tears or claiming he/she is the one being bullied and harassed.
- Constantly tries, and will do almost anything, to be in the spotlight.

Effective teaching strategies

- Within reasonable limits, do not respond to attention-seeking behaviour by giving attention, as this will unintentionally reinforce it. For example, if a pupil is being disruptive, he/she gets the teacher's attention – even if it is negative attention.
- Deal with the behaviour in as swift and impersonal a manner as possible with minimal speech and eye contact.
- Since a pupil displaying attention-seeking behaviour wants attention, provide him/her with positive reinforcement every time he/she does behave appropriately.
- Make a point of reinforcing the desirable behaviour of other pupils, e.g. praising those pupils who are lined up in a quiet and orderly manner, rather than chastising the pupil who is causing a disruption.
- Make sure that there are preventive strategies in place for dealing with disruptive behaviour, e.g. if you sense that the pupil is upset or is getting frustrated, help him/her get over the frustrating part of the work, invite the pupil to work together with a classmate or get him/her to help you with an errand. In other words, try distraction rather than confrontation.
- An egg-timer placed in front of the pupil can be useful for keeping the pupil focused and more likely to remain seated.
- Seat the pupil apart from other pupils who are likely to reinforce attention-seeking behaviour. Seat him/her near pupils who will ignore or be unaffected by poor behaviour.
- Catch the pupil being good (however minor). Look out for good behaviour and/or work and show approval.
- Make sure the pupil knows exactly what he/she is being praised for – 'I am really

pleased with you because…', rather than well-meaning but empty comments such as 'Good boy' and 'Well done'.

- Use the broken record technique for giving instructions. First, give the instruction as an 'I' statement. Listen to any objections. Reassert the original demands as necessary.

- Neutrally describe the behaviour which you want the pupil to stop, e.g. 'When you speak out while someone else is talking, no one can really listen to you. I would like you to wait your turn.'

- Special time:
    - Tell the pupil that he/she will be getting a special time each day.
    - Each day, tell him/her that special time will start in … minutes.
    - Tell the pupil that special time will start now.
    - Undertake special time.
    - Tell the pupil that special time will end in … minutes.
    - Tell the pupil that special time will end now.

The pupil has therefore been told several times that he/she is getting special time. During special time, the pupil may choose to do anything that is reasonable. Do not teach; simply watch the pupil, helping if, and only when, he/she requests it; never offer. Watch the pupil, and every so often sum up what the pupil is doing and praise the skills shown. This shows that the adult is paying attention. Do this daily. Do not, under any circumstances, take away the special time as a sanction; even if the pupil has had a bad day, still do special time.

Excessive motor activity (hyperactivity)

Characteristics

- Blurts out answers before questions have been completed.
- Interrupts or intrudes on others; has difficulty in waiting his/her turn.
- Behaviour is excessively energetic, inappropriate, and not goal-directed.
- Has difficulty sitting still or staying in one place.
- Excessive talking, moving, running and climbing about.
- Constantly 'on the go'.
- Throws tantrums.
- Runs about the room; climbs on furniture.
- Demands attention.
- Fidgets, fiddles, squirms, taps, pokes and kicks.
- Is talkative and noisy.

Effective teaching strategies

- Clearly establish classroom rules and expectations. Plan ahead for changes in routine or transitions and personally supervise these times.

- A pupil with hyperactive or impulsive behaviour will have difficulty sitting still. Instead of always trying to stop excessive movement, some productive physical movement should be incorporated into lessons, e.g. allowing the pupil to take the register to the school office. Sometimes simply being allowed to stand at his/her table while completing class work can be effective. Activities need to be carefully managed in order to minimise potential opportunities for misbehaviour.

- It is important to alternate activities that require the pupil to be seated with other activities that allow movement, e.g. maths and science investigations. It is also important to bear in mind that on some days it will be more difficult for the pupil to sit still than others. Thus teachers need to be flexible and modify instructional demands accordingly.

- Teach pupils to routinely check their own work before handing it in or seeking equipment – this will help them to develop self-checking strategies and to improve rushed or careless work.

- Be alert for early signs of increased restlessness and have diversionary strategies in place, e.g. games, puzzles.

- If the pupil does 'lose control' he/she will need somewhere safe and quiet where he/she can regain control without been watched by other pupils.

Impulsivity

Characteristics

- Flits between different activities, never finishing any.
- Acts or speaks without thinking; calls out; answers questions before they are finished.
- Cannot wait turn in group work or games.
- Is clumsy/accident prone, breaks things and accidentally hurts others.
- Cannot sit and listen to a story.
- Makes inappropriate remarks.

Effective teaching strategies

- Rewards and sanctions will be effective only if they are implemented immediately.
- Class rules should be clear and simple. They should also be phrased in a positive rather than a negative manner, e.g. instead of 'Don't run', use 'Please walk'.
- When it is necessary to reprimand a pupil for misbehaviour, this should be done privately. It is also of vital importance that the pupil understands that it is the behaviour that is being criticised and not the pupil.
- Praise, and positively reinforce, desirable behaviour – this can be done either publicly or privately.
- Seat the pupil near the teacher and surround him/her with positive role models.
- When work has been set, encourage the pupil to verbalise what must be done; first aloud to the teacher, so the teacher can clarify that the pupil has correctly understood the instructions, then quietly to him/herself, and finally, silently in his/her head.
- Teach the pupil self-checking strategies aimed at reducing impulsive behaviour, e.g. STAR (Stop, Think, Act, Review).

Non-compliant behaviour

Characteristics

- Refuses to comply with class/school rules/instructions.
- Displays defiant and/or disruptive behaviour in and out of the classroom.
- Displays tantrums and emotional outbursts.
- Has a low tolerance threshold.
- Appears resistant to change.
- Shows a lack of respect for others and/or others' property.
- Verbally abusive towards peers and/or staff.
- Sometimes hurts others and/or damages their work.

Effective teaching strategies

- Compliant behaviour is more likely to happen in a secure context where positive reinforcement is the norm.
- Behavioural expectations should be made clear to the pupil. Such a discussion should be initiated at the beginning of an academic year and not following a specific incident. The pupil should also be involved in selecting the most appropriate rewards/sanctions.
- Praise and reinforce compliant behaviours.
- As far as is realistically possible, try to ignore inappropriate behaviours.
- Provide immediate feedback about acceptable and unacceptable behaviours, but be aware of the ratio of positive versus negative feedback.
- Draw compliant behaviour to the attention of other staff so that they can also reinforce positive behaviours.
- Direct your time and effort to those pupils presenting appropriate behaviours.
- Spot the pupil who is conforming, and reward immediately and spontaneously.
- Respond in a calm and composed manner when boundaries are crossed.
- Teach the pupil strategies to deal with difficult situations.
- Involve the pupil in self-monitoring.

Poor social skills

Characteristics

- Lack of social competence includes difficulty accepting criticism, receiving compliments, saying no and giving positive feedback.
- Inability to understand social cues.
- Low social status among peers.
- Difficulty building/maintaining interpersonal relationships.
- Withdrawn behaviour.
- Verbal and/or physical aggression.
- Temper tantrums.
- Difficulty dealing with social and academic problems.

Effective teaching strategies

- Peer relationships can be improved through specific social skills programmes, e.g. Circle Time or Circle of Friends activities.
- Encourage and praise appropriate social behaviour.
- Incorporate the elements of effective communication, participation and co-operation into curriculum planning and preparation.
- Encourage, but do not force, the pupil's participation in collaborative learning tasks with other pupils.
- Maximise the opportunities to show praise and approval in an attempt to increase the pupil's self-esteem within the classroom.
- Emphasise the pupil's academic strengths by creating co-operative learning situations in which reading skills, vocabulary, memory and so on may be viewed as assets by peers, thereby engendering acceptance.
- If the lesson involves pairing off or choosing partners, use some arbitrary means of pairing, or ask an especially kind pupil if he/she would agree to choose him/her as a partner before the pairing takes place.
- The pupil might benefit from a 'buddy system'. Sensitive classmates could be seated next to the pupil and could 'look out' for him/her and attempt to include the pupil in school activities.
- Foster the pupil's involvement with others. Encourage active socialisation and limit time spent alone. For example, a support assistant seated at the lunch table could actively encourage the pupil to participate in the conversation of his/her peers, not only by soliciting the pupil's opinions and asking him/her questions but also by subtly reinforcing other children who do the same.
- Provide structured play opportunities, e.g. encouraging the pupil to play a board game with one or two others not only structures play but also offers an opportunity to practise social skills.

Lowered self-esteem

Effective teaching strategies

- A whole-school approach is needed to boost and maintain self-esteem in all pupils.
- A pupil with lowered self-esteem requires a learning environment in which he/she is able to view him/herself as a competent and productive member of the class.
- Poor self-esteem can be improved through specific social skills programmes and by using self-esteem-raising activities.
- Improving a pupil's self-esteem should involve all those concerned with the pupil, especially the parents.
- Give frequent and repeated reassurance and encouragement. Praise should focus on pupils' talents and accomplishments (whatever they may be) by providing opportunities for these to be shown, e.g. in a celebration assembly.

Pen portraits and sample IEPs

Pen portrait of Jenny Smith

Jenny is four years old. She is healthy, but large for her age. She is the eldest of two. Jenny and her brother attended Sure Start groups, and a nursery nurse is working on play at home on a weekly basis with Jenny's brother. Jenny has the potential to do well but lacks guidance, concentration and focus. Jenny finds it difficult to complete an activity unless constantly encouraged. She is very fidgety and distractible and is always looking at what else is going on.

Key Stage 2

Pen portrait of Joe Dent

Joe is nine-and-a-half years old. He does not have learning difficulties but finds it hard to stay in his seat, attend to the class teacher and conform to class rules. He takes offence very easily and will run out of class whenever he feels slighted. Joe also frequently makes loud, spontaneous and inappropriate comments, which are disruptive in class and distracting to the teacher and other pupils, as well as often being hurtful.

Key Stage 3

Pen portrait of Mark Tyler

Mark is a Year 9 pupil who has moderate learning difficulties. He finds it hard to cope with the large number of curricular and social demands made in secondary school and he disrupts lessons, refusing to apply himself to classroom tasks. He is unable to accept criticism and responds angrily, running out of classes and causing trouble around school. Mark has a good sense of humour and does respond well to humour from others.

For a blank IEP form see Appendix 8.

Early Years Action/Early Years Action Plus
Individual Education Plan

Name: Jenny Smith	**Date of birth:** 3/5/1999
Date: 1/5/200…	**Review date:** September 200…

Nature of pupil's difficulties: Has difficulty concentrating on activities. Finds it hard to share and take turns, and it has been known for her to physically harm others or break equipment.

Targets	Strategies	Resources	Evaluation
To improve Jenny's listening and attention skills so that with no more than two other peers in withdrawal she can complete a simple game with support, waiting her turn and maintaining concentration.	Withdrawal to quiet room (maximum of two children with adult support). Use of wait/listen/look Xs, turn and praise desired behaviour, listening, looking and waiting.	SENCO Simple board game Two peers	Jenny following rules and waiting for peers to take their turn.
To complete simple jigsaw, drawing, sorting activities without adult prompts.	Adult to teach Jenny to complete simple making/sorting activities individually and then in a pair. Skills learned are then to be encouraged generally in the classroom.	SENCO Range of matching, sorting, early counting activities One other peer	Skills taught individually generalised to classroom without adult prompts, link to target.
To use equipment safely and not endanger other children.	To play alongside or with other children in role play outdoors without need for adult intervention.	Home corner Equipment Outdoor play area and equipment	Jenny with other children outside or in home corner without conflict or complaint for five minutes. Link to target 1.

Parental involvement: Ask mum and dad to spend five minutes each day looking at book or pictures and encouraging Jenny to describe things.

School Action/School Action Plus
Individual Education Plan

Name: Joe Dent
Date: 1/5/2004

Date of birth: 9/10/1994
Review date: September 200...

Nature of pupil's difficulties: Finds it difficult to remain in class. Finds it difficult to relate to group instructions and act upon them. Does not empathise with others or acknowledge that others have views and feelings.

Targets	Strategies	Resources	Evaluation
Joe to remain in the class for entire lesson.	Joe to have an individual timetable. Tasks to be short and chunked, and to be given to CSA upon completion.	Work station Visual timetable Work baskets Access to CSA time	Joe to remain in class (not run out of door for one lesson).
Joe to put his hand up to make a comment to the teacher.	Joe to be taught strategy and to practise it on a 1:1 with teacher and CSA before being asked to use it in class. Joe to be shown a red card if he shouts out by mistake.	CSA and teacher Time Red Card Green Card	Reduction in shouting out by three times by end of week.
Joe to work with a peer in a co-operative manner.	Joe to be taught how to operate a computer program and then to teach a peer how to operate it. Joe to do this without negative comments.	Teacher time Computer program Peer	Peer to have learned how to operate program without Joe insulting him.

Parental involvement: Joe to sit and work on a two-minute homework task of Joe's choosing without getting out of his seat, starting a conversation or distracting mum. Mum to reward if this is achieved.

School Action/School Action Plus
Individual Education Plan

Name: Mark Tyler
Date: November 2000…

Date of birth: 20/12/1989
Review date: March 200…

Nature of pupil's difficulties: Mark is unwilling to apply himself to classroom tasks even when they are appropriate to his level of working. At such times Mark's behaviour can be impossible to manage, resulting in disruption and rampages around school.

Targets	Strategies	Resources	Evaluation
Be able to sit in class and complete tasks for all lessons.	Support with tasks. Rewards for skills shown.	Classroom assistant	Pupil planner. Self-assessment. Staff reports.
Be able to work and socialise in a small group of peers.	Achievable, planned tasks and extra work as control mechanism (e.g. word search, collage).	Pack of work – topic packs – activity packs	
Improve self-esteem.	Verbal praise, individual attention, certificates, positive reports home, display of work, special responsibilities.	Display work space	
Improve confidence.	Identification of significant person to offer regular support.	Classroom assistant. Year tutor/subject teacher time	Staff, parent and pupil's views.
Start to use phonic/contextual cues.	2 x weekly 1:1 work on spelling – teaching activities and games. Liaison with curricular teachers to reinforce essential vocabulary and spellings.	Toe by Toe Dyspraxia pack IT program	Testing/reading and spelling records. Pupil evaluation. Classroom generalisation.

Parental involvement: Set time for homework. Praise for success. Communication via homework diary. Attendance at half-termly reviews.

Section 5

Medically diagnosed behavioural difficulties

Attention Deficit Hyperactivity Disorder (ADHD)

ADHD describes a pupil who is inattentive, hyperactive and impulsive. For a diagnosis to be given, certain characteristics must be met (as determined by the Diagnostic and Statistical Manual of the American Psychiatric Association). These are described below. These behaviours should appear before the age of seven, continue for at least six months, appear in a variety of settings, and impair the ability to make social and educational progress.

- Pupils with ADHD may also have difficulty with personal organisation and fine motor skills.
- Pupils may be without friends, fail to reach academic potential and are in lots of trouble with adults, often resulting in low self-esteem.
- As yet the reasons for ADHD have not been proven, although it may be caused by a chemical imbalance in the brain.
- Medication can be prescribed which may improve the condition.
- The incidence in the population is between 0.5 per cent and 1 per cent of the childhood population, although it is thought to be increasing.
- ADHD can run in families.
- About half of children diagnosed as having ADHD will have difficulties through to adulthood.

Characteristics

Inattention

- Fails to give close attention to detail.
- Has difficulty sustaining attention.
- Finds it difficult to listen to instructions.
- Very distractible.
- Difficulty organising tasks and activities.
- Finds difficulty completing a task.
- Reluctant to engage in tasks that require sustained mental effort.
- Is forgetful in daily activities.

N.B. Pupils should display six or more characteristics from the first list above or six or more from the combined hyperactivity and impulsivity lists.

The diagnosis cannot be applied to any child who appears naughty or difficult, or who may daydream.

Medication

It is thought that ADHD develops because a child's brain does not receive the correct amount of natural chemicals. Some pupils with ADHD may be prescribed medication by a consultant. Medication works by stimulating the production of these chemicals. It also helps to absorb any excess.

Medication has to be monitored for a period of time after prescription in order to achieve the correct dosage. Schools may need to be a part of this monitoring process.

There may be side effects associated with medication; nervousness and sleeping difficulties suggest the need for adjustment of the dose or indicate that it should be taken at a different time. Other side effects include loss of appetite, which may result in weight loss, drowsiness, tics, headache, dizziness or blurred vision.

It is essential that medication is taken as prescribed at set times, which may have implications for schools. Consideration should be given to this if pupils are to stay for school lunch, or take part in school visits or residential trips.

Medication prescribed to pupils with ADHD is a controlled drug, which should be kept in a locked cabinet.

Medication can be effective for certain pupils.

It will:

- improve attention to people and tasks;
- decrease impulsivity;
- decrease reaction to situations;
- decrease activity levels.

It does not:

- teach good behaviour;
- teach social and academic skills which have been previously missed (social and academic);
- teach the ability to deal with feelings;
- motivate the pupil.

Prader-Willi syndrome

The incidence of Prader-Willi syndrome is approximately 1 in every 15,000 births and it occurs in both males and females. Pupils may exhibit some or none of the following characteristics:

- Hyperphagia (excessive appetite) caused by a failure in the mechanism, which tells a person that they have had sufficient food. Between the ages of one and four, interest in food increases and it can become an obsession. Some children can control food intake, but others eat at every opportunity, whether it be appropriate or not, e.g. taking other people's food, eating food from bins.
- Behaviour which can include temper outbursts, resistance to change, obsessive and/or compulsive behaviour, possessiveness of items to which they are attached, stubbornness.
- Social skills may be restricted and may need to be taught; relationships with adults are usually good.
- Perseveration can occur, which is persistent talking or questioning about a topic.
- Skin-picking can become obsessive, and due to high pain thresholds the pupil may not feel any discomfort. An increase in this activity can be related to stress.
- Other difficulties may be present: hypotonia (low muscle tone); short stature; hypogonadism which causes delayed or arrested puberty; limited temperature control; high pain threshold; eyesight problems; curvature of the spine; dental or oral problems; speech and language delay; cognitive ability varying from moderate to severe learning difficulty to a learning ability within the average range.

Strategies to support the pupil

- Give firm, consistent, but caring, discipline.
- Deal with temper tantrums by:
  - being able to identify the signs and diffusing the situation;
  - removing the pupil from a potential audience as he/she may play to this;
  - remaining calm;
  - avoiding rewarding the behaviour by giving what was asked for;
  - identifying triggers and, if possible, avoiding them; discussing the issue when calm has been restored.
- Anxiety related to change:
  - provide predictable routines with warning of any changes that are to take place;
  - use a visual timetable to show the routine of the day.

- Teach social skills:
    - turn-taking skills through games; lotto; taking turns to roll a ball to each other; small-group work to take turns to make comments.
    - participate in Circle Time.
- Perseveration:
    - use picture cue cards to indicate when a pupil should not shout out;
    - give a limit to how many times a pupil may ask a question.
- Skin-picking:
    - praise and reward for not picking the skin;
    - be aware that it could be a sign of increased anxiety.
- Ensure strategies are in place to maintain self-esteem.

Tourette's syndrome

The full name of the condition is Gilles de la Tourette's Syndrome, after the doctor who initially recognised the characteristics of the condition. It is usually known as Tourette's syndrome or TS.

Characteristics

- TS is caused by problems with the development of the central nervous system.
- It runs in families, but which genes are involved is not known.
- It usually begins in childhood or teenage years, the most difficult times being between ages eight and thirteen.
- Tics can take several forms:
    - the simple form being twitches or blinks;
    - vocal tics being grunts or swearing;
    - more complex forms being movements such as squatting while walking, twirling round, touching objects or people, repeating phrases.
- Tics can give the appearance of being done intentionally. However, they are involuntary movements which cannot be controlled. Even if they are suppressed for a short time, the pupil will need to let out the movement. Some may learn to do it in a private place.
- Pupils may have good or bad days.
- One behaviour may fade to be replaced by another.
- There are other difficulties: obsessive-compulsive problems, attention difficulties, hyperactivity, impulsiveness, aggressive behaviour, movement co-ordination difficulties, sleep disturbance and educational difficulties.
- Mild problems may decrease with age.
- Some cases of TS remain undiagnosed because symptoms are mild and decrease as the child grows up.
- Drug treatment may be used when the problems are more severe.
- It may be possible for psychologists to teach strategies and techniques in order to reduce some of the undesired behaviours.

Many pupils with Tourette's syndrome may be inattentive, hyperactive and impulsive. They may also have problems with social skills, making it difficult to make and retain friendships.

Strategies to support pupils with Tourette's syndrome

- Pupils should not be criticised for being unable to control themselves.
- Ignore behaviours which are not seriously disruptive.
- Allow pupils to go to an agreed safe place when under stress.
- Encourage peers to develop an understanding of the TS condition. It may be possible for the pupil with TS to discuss how his condition makes him feel in PSHE.
- Encourage participation in out-of-school clubs, activities (with support if necessary).
- Consider ways of developing self-esteem, e.g. giving jobs, fostering the pupil's strengths.
- Understand that the condition may fluctuate in its intensity.
- Pupils may talk at inappropriate times, interrupt and appear not to listen. Give tape recorders to use; point out to pupils the most important facts to be learned; give reminders of tasks to be done.
- Reduce levels of work to be completed if tics interrupt the output of work.
- See strategies in previous chapters to address issues related to ADHD.

Appendices

SEN legislation impacting on current practice

In the Education Acts of 1993 and 1996, Parliament sought to highlight the rights of children with special educational needs.

The 1993 Act stated that, as a general principle, children with special educational needs should ideally be educated in mainstream schools, if that was what the parents wanted. There were many conditions attached; for instance, the mainstream school's ability to ensure the child received the necessary provision while ensuring the efficient education of others. The result was that many children, who could have benefited from inclusion, were denied access to a mainstream education.

In 1994, The Salamanca Statement, drawn up by a UNESCO world conference, asked all governments to 'adopt as a matter of law or policy, the principle of inclusive education, enrolling all children in regular schools, unless there are compelling reasons for doing otherwise'.

In 1997 the government published *Excellence for All Children – Meeting Special Educational Needs*. In this, the educational, social and moral benefits of inclusive education were stressed.

The DfEE Circular 10/98, Section 550A of the Education Act 1996: 'the use of force to control or restrain pupils', gives examples of circumstances in which physical intervention might be appropriate, and factors that teachers should bear in mind when deciding whether to intervene.

In 1998, *Meeting Special Educational Needs – A Programme of Action* was published. This made the link with the Disability Rights Taskforce, which produced a report entitled *From Exclusion to Inclusion* in 1999. This report recommended: 'A strengthened right for parents of children with statements of special educational need to a place in a mainstream school.'

The Special Educational Needs and Disability Act of 2001 amended the 1996 Education Act and is a positive endorsement of inclusion. Parental choice, be it a special school or a mainstream preference, must be taken into consideration.

The *Index of Inclusion: Developing Learning and Participation in Schools* (2000) is concerned with improving educational attainments through inclusive practice.

The Revised SEN Code of Practice on the Identification and Assessment of Pupils with Special Educational Needs came into force in 2001, and there has been a wealth of DfES guidance on the subject of effective inclusion of all children and young people into mainstream school settings.

In 2002, the Audit Commission Report: *Special Educational Needs – A Mainstream Issue*, highlighted challenges to schools.

The 2003 Behaviour and Attendance Strategy aimed to promote good behaviour and attendance in schools.

Published in 2003, *Guidance on the Use of Restrictive Physical Interventions for Staff Working with Children and Adults* provides guidance on the use of restrictive physical intervention for children and adults.

Removing Barriers to Achievement: The Government's Strategy for SEN (2004) looks at issues surrounding the care of children with SEN.

2004 – the instigation of an Inclusive Development Programme, linking Education, Health, Social Services and the Voluntary Sector in order to build models of good practice.

Social skills resources

Circle Time

Circle Time Resources – George Robinson and Barbara Maines, Lucky Duck Publishing.

Solution-focused approaches

www.enabling.com: *Crucial Skills* – Penny Johnson and Tina Rae, Lucky Duck Publishing.

Anger management

Anger Management – Adrian Faupel, Elizabeth Herrick and Peter Sharp, David Fulton Publishers.

Support groups/friendship groups

Developing Pupils' Social Communication Skills: Practical Resources – Penny Barratt, Julie Border and Helen Joy, David Fulton Publishers.

'Buddy' systems.

Peer listening

Listen and Hear – Hull City Psychological Service, Tel: 01482 613390.

Curriculum-based approaches

Ideas and resources may be gained from pandoraproject.co.uk

The Emotional Literacy Handbook: Promoting Whole School Strategies – Antidote/David Fulton Publishers.

Dealing with Feeling: An Emotional Literacy Curriculum – Tina Rae, Lucky Duck Publishing.

Pastoral Support Plan

Name: Paul Brown	DOB: 01.01.98
Year Group: 4	Class: 4P
SEN Code of Practice Stage: School Action Plus	Looked After Child: No

Date of PSP meeting: 04.03.0…

Date for implementation of plan: 07.03.0…

Dates for next meeting: 21/03/0….

People invited to attend PSP meeting:		Present
Pupil:	Paul Brown	Y
Parents/carers:	Mrs Brown (mother)	Y
School staff:	Mrs Stock (Head teacher)	Y
	Mrs Dibley (PSP & SEN Co-ordinator)	Y
	Mr Haden (Class teacher)	Y
LEA representatives:	Ms Branton (Educational Psychologist)	Y
Other agencies:		

Background/additional information

According to Paul, within school he particularly enjoys ICT and DT. He recently received a Head teacher's award for his last DT project. Out of school, Paul's main interests are playing on his computer and play station and he enjoys football with his older teenage brothers. Paul's parents have recently separated, and there is conflict between them – Paul has not seen his father for some months.

Reasons for drawing up the PSP

In class Paul often exhibits disruptive behaviour, making noises and so on (this is particularly noticeable when he is required to work co-operatively with others or listen for extended periods of time). Within class Paul's behaviour is well managed by his teachers. In more unstructured activities Paul is becoming more aggressive towards his peers and extremely oppositional to adults. Many strategies have been tried including behaviour charts and giving him extra responsibilities. As a result of Paul kicking a dinner lady, and on a separate occasion punching one of his peers in the face, Paul has had two fixed-term exclusions. In spite of this he is not an unpopular child; the children do like to play with him, as he organises the games. When Paul feels children have broken rules, he can become aggressive. At the present time Paul's Mum has chosen to take him home for lunch. In the past Paul has responded well to visual prompts. Social stories have also been used but have proved unsuccessful.

Aims of PSP

To attempt to prevent further fixed-term exclusions. To integrate Paul fully into the lunchtime session. To reduce the number of aggressive incidents.

Identified needs

Behavioural	Paul needs to know what behaviour is appropriate at playtimes and lunchtimes. He responds well to stickers and stamps. Social stories have been tried but SENCO is inexperienced in using them.
	Paul needs to learn to take turns.
Learning	Very bright and is in top sets but is underachieving.
Social	Paul needs help with understanding the situation with his parents.
Emotional	Paul is experiencing a difficult time due to the separation of his parents – he needs an available adult and encouragement to talk to when upset or angry rather than hurting another pupil.

SMART targets

- To learn to keep his hands and feet to himself
- To take turns in a game
- To walk away if someone makes him cross

Action

School	To provide adult support at lunchtime for a short period of time. Paul to have his lunchtime divided into sections: lunch, game on the yard, quieter games inside with a friend. Stamps to be put on a behaviour chart for appropriate behaviour in each section, leading up to a negotiated reward at the end of the week, e.g. time on the computer.

	SENCO to seek training in social stories. Mr Haden to provide quiet game time and to use this opportunity to chat with Paul.
Pupil	To discuss the benefits of playing co-operatively and to talk to an adult when others break rules. Paul has agreed to the reward scheme.
Parents	Mum to speak to school staff at the end of the day. Parents to reward Paul if he gets sufficient stamps at the end of the week. Mum to discuss effects of conflict on Paul with dad and attempt to establish contact.
Educational Psychologist	To carry out lunchtime observations and make recommendations. Rewards and sanctions.

Rewards and sanctions

School	Stamp chart	Paul to be supervised in a quiet room for the remainder of lunchtime if he hurts another pupil. If this happens more than twice weekly then Paul goes home for lunch the next day.
Home	Pocket money; small treats	No pocket money/treats.

Monitoring arrangements

Mrs Dibley (SENCO) to speak to Paul before lunch to reinforce any positive behaviours demonstrated throughout the morning, and to remind him of the type of behaviour expected of him at lunchtime.

Mr Haden (class teacher) to look at the number of stamps given at lunchtime and to discuss the positives and negatives from lunchtime prior to afternoon lessons. Mr Haden to liaise with Mum at the end of the day.

Ms Branton (Educational Psychologist) to attend next PSP.

Pastoral Support Plan

Name:	DOB:
Year Group:	Class:
SEN Code of Practice stage:	Looked-after child:

Date of PSP meeting:
Date for implementation of plan:
Dates for next meeting:

People invited to attend PSP meeting:		Present
Pupil:		
Parents/carers:		
School staff:		
LEA representatives:		
Other agencies:		

Background/additional information

Reasons for drawing up PSP

Identified needs:

Behavioural	
Learning	
Social	
Emotional	

SMART targets

Action:	
School	
Pupil	
Parents	
Educational Psychologist	

Rewards and sanctions:	
School	
Home	

Monitoring arrangements

Physical intervention to control or restrain pupils

Guidance for schools

Although incidents necessitating the use of physical restraint on pupils will be relatively few in number, schools should be very clear about the set procedures involved.

The 1996 Education Act (Section 550A, paragraphs 9 and 10) allows:

> teachers and other persons who are authorised by the head teacher to have control or charge of pupils ... to use such force as is reasonable in all the circumstances to prevent a pupil from doing, or continuing to do, any of the following:

- Committing a criminal offence
- Injuring themselves or others
- Engaging in any behaviour prejudicial to maintaining good order.

DfES guidance on physical intervention in schools

- Schools should have a policy on physical intervention, cross-referenced to other relevant policies (SEN, Health and Safety, Behaviour and Discipline, Child Protection).

- The school policy should help staff to develop their understanding of the appropriate use of physical restraint, update restraint training, apply alternative defusing techniques and record an incident of physical intervention appropriately.

- All physical intervention training should be set within the context of skilled behaviour management, defusing techniques and conflict resolution.

- If a school assesses that there is likelihood that physical restraint will take place, training is imperative, at least for key staff members.

- Training should not be a one-off; it should involve regular refresher courses.

- Interventions of any kind, physical or not, always require that staff take into account the age, developmental level, understanding and cultural background of the child concerned.

- Physical Intervention or restraint is not a substitute for good discipline. Its use should be rare and it should never become habitual or routine.

- Planned physical intervention is not an act of aggression or anger. **Any force, beyond what is needed to prevent harm or injury to the child or others, is unreasonable**. A physical restraint should be a neutral experience, either punitive or pleasant.

- Restraint must be of minimum force to prevent further danger to the pupil, peers and adults.

- The subject should be reminded that the restraint is only temporary and clear instructions should be given as to what needs to be done in order to stop the intervention.

- Another member of staff should be present, not only to assist, but also to witness the incident and report on it afterwards. To this end staff should not be in situations that leave them alone in difficult circumstances.

- The use of seclusion is not appropriate. It is an offence to lock a child in a room without a Court Order, except in an emergency, while seeking assistance.

- In educational settings, double or high door handles can be used, or outside doors can be locked, for safety or security reasons when an adult is supervising.

Circular 10/98 states that parents should always be involved when an incident occurs. Parents should also be aware of the school's policy on restraint.

A physical intervention policy

A policy should:

- tie in with other relevant policies;
- explain to all staff when physical restraint would be appropriate (and when not);
- explain clearly the procedure before, during and after an incident;
- be clear about who has authority to use physical restraint;
- be accessible to all staff;
- be understood by parents and children;
- outline the circumstances when the Police or medical support should be called;
- clarify the reporting of the incident;
- outline procedures for informing parents about the restraint;
- ensure effective debriefing for the pupil, staff member and witness/witnesses;
- act as a stimulus to individual planning for the pupil involved;
- mention the complaints procedure for parents/pupils.

Physical restraints references

Inclusive Schooling: Children with Special Needs (2001). DfES Guidance.

Advice on Whole-School Behaviour and Attendance Policy (2003). DfES Guidance.

SEN Code of Practice on the Identification and Assessment of Pupils with Special Educational Needs. DfES.

Circular 10/98 – Section 550A of the Education Act 1996: the use of force to control or restrain pupils. DfEE.

Physical Intervention to Control or Restrain Pupils – Guidance for Schools (2002). Bath and NE Somerset Education Service.

The Special Educational Needs and Disability Act 2001.

Primary pupils: 30 examples of rewards and sanctions

+=+=+=+ Punched cards +=+=+=+

The pupil is given a special good behaviour card. At the end of the activity/day, the pupil's card is punched, to reward good behaviour. If the pupil achieves a previously agreed total, he/she receives an appropriate reward.

+=+=+=+ Pulling sticks +=+=+=+

Pupils earn up to five lolly sticks in one lesson. These are displayed on the pupil's desk. If the pupil receives all five sticks by the end of the lesson he/she is rewarded appropriately.

+=+=+=+ Hanging paper-clips +=+=+=+

Pupils earn paper-clips for good behaviour in order to make a chain of 20.

+=+=+=+ Jumping frogs +=+=+=+

Good class behaviour helps the frog to jump to a lily pad. If the pupil makes it to the end pad by a previously agreed time, a reward is given.

+=+=+=+ 1-2-3-4-5 +=+=+=+

When the pupil behaves well, a number is written on a laminated card that is placed on the pupil's desk. If the pupil continues to behave well and achieves 1-2-3-4-5 by the end of the lesson, he/she is rewarded appropriately.

+=+=+=+ Behaviour agreements/contracts +=+=+=+

Displayed in the classroom, these can act as a visual prompt and help to remind the pupil that his/her behaviour is the pupil's choice.

+=+=+=+ Scales +=+=+=+

A target number of marbles is put into a jar on one side of the scales; marbles are put into a jar on the other side as the pupils carry out desired behaviours. When the balance is achieved the class receives a reward.

+=+=+=+ Connect 4 +=+=+=+

Drop counters down. Get four in a line and the class gains a reward.

+=+=+=+ Golden time +=+=+=+

This is given when the class, cumulatively, gains points, and golden time is given at the end of the week. The activities, which are given as rewards, can be decided by the children making suggestions and the favourite for the week being voted upon. Activities could be making and eating toast, making plasticine models and so on.

+=+=+=+ Stars on the board +=+=+=+

Given for pupils who are observed to be behaving well, e.g. working on task or listening to the teacher. If the class earns sufficient stars then pupils have a few minutes' extra playtime.

+=+=+=+ Table rewards +=+=+=+

Given for the group of children at a particular table who have tidied their table well after a craft session or worked quietly during the session. They have a small treat determined by the teacher.

+=+=+=+ Golden table at lunchtime +=+=+=+

For pupils who have been chosen for good behaviour; being kind, trying hard, listening to a story.

+=+=+=+ Star tubs +=+=+=+

These are placed on a table and have a star put in as the teacher observes good working practice. The table with the most stars by a certain time gains a reward.

+=+=+=+ Attendance cup +=+=+=+

The class with the best attendance of the week gains the cup and a 15-minute treat.

+=+=+=+ Modelling good behaviour +=+=+=+

This is a way to remind some pupils of what they should be doing and to praise others for appropriate behaviour. Comments such as 'Oh, look, John and Emily are picking up the cubes' may encourage more tidying up; 'Paul has written two lines already' may spur others to more writing.

+=+=+=+ Over-the-top comments +=+=+=+

Making positive comments, which appear slightly 'over the top' but give pupils a boost. 'How did you do this; it's so good?'; 'How are you always getting so many ticks on your work?'

+=+=+=+ Star of the day +=+=+=+

A particular pupil's photograph is displayed in a 'frame' with a comment underneath stating why he/she is a star. The credit could be given for good work, being especially kind to a classmate or listening well. The whole class could make suggestions or the teacher could make the choice.

+=+=+=+ Helper of the day +=+=+=+

The pupil could have his/her photograph placed on the wall.

+=+=+=+ Helping with class pets +=+=+=+

Could be a reward.

+=+=+=+ Earning a treat +=+=+=+

Identify what the pupil enjoys through observation or by asking him/her what he/she likes doing. The pupil has to earn points through a jointly agreed scheme for achieving an appropriate behaviour, e.g. putting up his/her hand, not shouting out, remaining in his/her seat. The points could be recorded on a chart, and if the agreed amount is collected the pupil receives a 'treat'. It may be necessary to 'treat' often in the initial period and slowly build up the time that the pupil has to achieve the desired behaviour.

+=+=+=+ Quick notes +=+=+=+

or a small certificate given by the class teacher on an *ad hoc* or regular basis for any behaviour that represents an achievement for a particular child.

+=+=+=+ Courtesy cards +=+=+=+

Given by members of staff to pupils who are observed being polite and well behaved when moving around school.

+=+=+=+ Good news phone calls +=+=+=+

Made to parents about their child (sometimes parents hear only negative news about their children).

+=+=+=+ Head teacher's award +=+=+=+

A special sticker or certificate given by the head teacher for an achievement by a child.

+=+=+=+ Certificate assembly +=+=+=+

Letters are sent home to parents to invite them to a special assembly where certificates to commend good behaviour are given out. The parents and children are then invited to have drinks and biscuits after the assembly.

+=+=+=+ Star of the week +=+=+=+

Chosen from the whole school, or one from each class. The pupils' photograph is displayed on a noticeboard and a report about him/her appears in the weekly school newspaper.

+=+=+=+ Reward cards +=+=+=+

of varying types: apple trees, ladybirds, dinosaurs with outlines for spots to be put on, when the pupil carries out the required, agreed behaviour.

+=+=+=+ Balancing scales +=+=+=+

Use a set of balancing scales and some colourful weights. One side of the scale represents good/positive behaviour, and the other side represents less than desirable behaviour. Pupils attempt to keep the scale in balance or weighted to the positive side. Weights may be added to reinforce specific incidents, or whenever a lesson or activity is completed.

+=+=+=+ Traffic-light cards +=+=+=+

The pupil will need a red, yellow and green card. These should be pinned on the classroom wall. If a pupil behaves inappropriately he/she is asked to pull the green card off the wall, leaving the yellow card exposed. If the yellow card must be pulled off, leaving the red card exposed, the pupil receives a previously agreed sanction, e.g. five minutes of time out. If the red card must be pulled off, the pupil gets a slightly more severe sanction, e.g. ten minutes of time out. If at the end of a lesson the pupil has retained his/her green card a suitable reward is given.

+=+=+=+ Card system – 3 colours +=+=+=+

Top card = green; two crosses = yellow; two more crosses = red; two more = no card. The pupil can earn any number of good behaviour points on yellow and green. If a pupil earns five behaviour points out of a possible seven, he/she has the choice of a reward or to fast-track to green the next day.

Early years: examples of rewards

[:[:[:[:[:[:[:[:[: Golden cushion :]:]:]:]:]:]:]:]:]

Children are chosen to sit on the cushions after demonstrating some feature of good behaviour or special trait.

[:[:[:[:[:[:[:[:[: Colourful kites :]:]:]:]:]:]:]:]:]

Draw a kite. The pupil earns tails for his/her kite. Attach the tails to the string of the paper kite.

[:[:[:[:[:[:[:[:[: Fill the flower box :]:]:]:]:]:]:]:]:]

Label a plastic planting trough with the words 'Beautiful Behaviour in Bloom'. The pupil earns paper flowers to put in his/her classroom garden.

[:[:[:[:[:[:[:[:[: Marbles in a jar :]:]:]:]:]:]:]:]:]

Start with two jars. One jar is empty; the other jar is filled with marbles. The pupil's first step is to earn ten marbles. Reward positive behaviours by taking a marble out of the full jar and dropping it into the empty jar. When the tenth marble has been earned, the pupil 'earns' a previously agreed reward. No marbles may be taken away. After the pupil has earned the ten marbles, they are put back into the first jar and the process starts again. The number of marbles may be increased if appropriate.

[:[:[:[:[:[:[:[:[: Modelling good behaviour :]:]:]:]:]:]:]:]:]

A way to remind some pupils of what they should be doing and praise others for appropriate behaviour. Comments such as 'Oh, look, John and Emily are picking up the cubes' may encourage more tidying up; 'Paul has written two lines already' may spur others to more writing.

[:[:[:[:[:[:[:[: Helper of the day :]:]:]:]:]:]:]:]:]:]

He/she could have his/her photograph placed on the wall.

[:[:[:[:[:[:[:[: Over-the-top comments :]:]:]:]:]:]:]:]:]:]

Making positive comments which appear slightly 'over the top' but give pupils a boost. 'How did you do this, it's so good?'; 'How are you always getting so many ticks on your work?'

[:[:[:[:[:[:[:[: Star of the day :]:]:]:]:]:]:]:]:]:]

A particular pupil's photograph is displayed in a 'frame' with a comment underneath stating why he/she is a star. The credit could be given for good work, being especially kind to a classmate or listening well. The whole class could make suggestions or the teacher could make the choice.

[:[:[:[:[:[:[:[: Quick notes :]:]:]:]:]:]:]:]:]

or a small certificate given by the class teacher on an *ad hoc* or regular basis for any behaviour that is an achievement for a particular child.

[:[:[:[:[:[:[:[: Head teacher's award :]:]:]:]:]:]:]:]:]

A special sticker or certificate given by the head teacher for an achievement by a child.

[:[:[:[:[:[:[:[: Certificate assembly :]:]:]:]:]:]:]:]:]

Letters are sent home to parents to invite them to a special assembly where certificates to commend good behaviour are given out. The parents and children are then invited to have drinks and biscuits after the assembly.

[:[:[:[:[:[:[:[: Reward cards :]:]:]:]:]:]:]:]:]

of varying types: apple trees, ladybirds, dinosaurs with outlines for spots to be put on. Given when the pupil carries out the required, agreed behaviour.

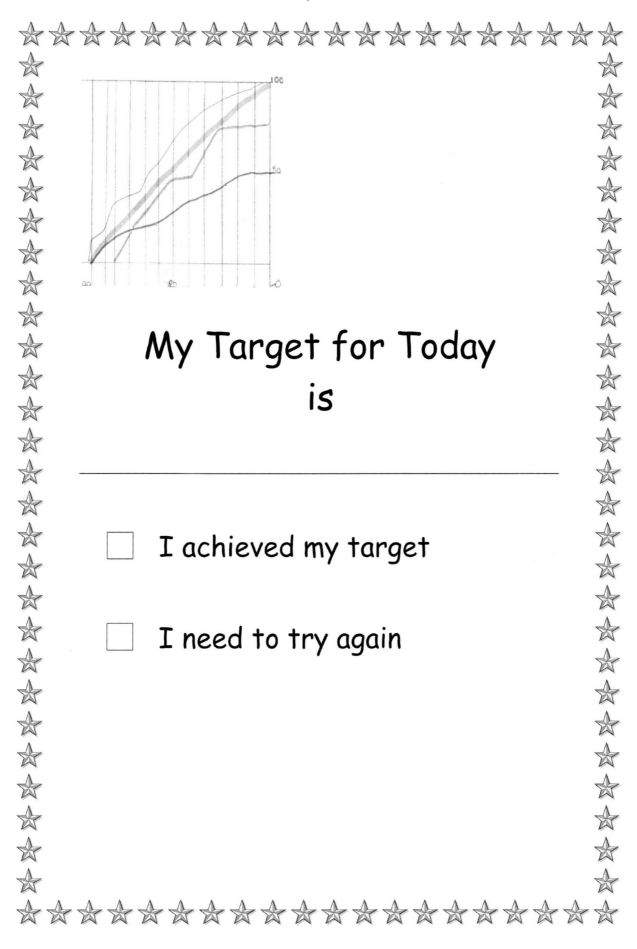

My Target for Today
is

_____

☐   I achieved my target

☐   I need to try again

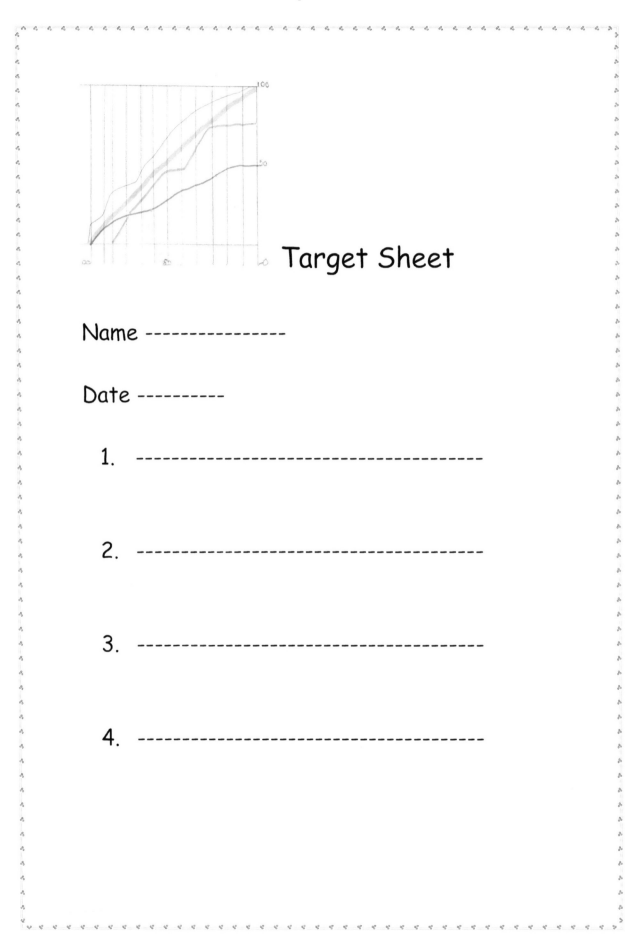

Target Sheet

Name -----------------

Date ----------

1. ---------------------------------------

2. ---------------------------------------

3. ---------------------------------------

4. ---------------------------------------

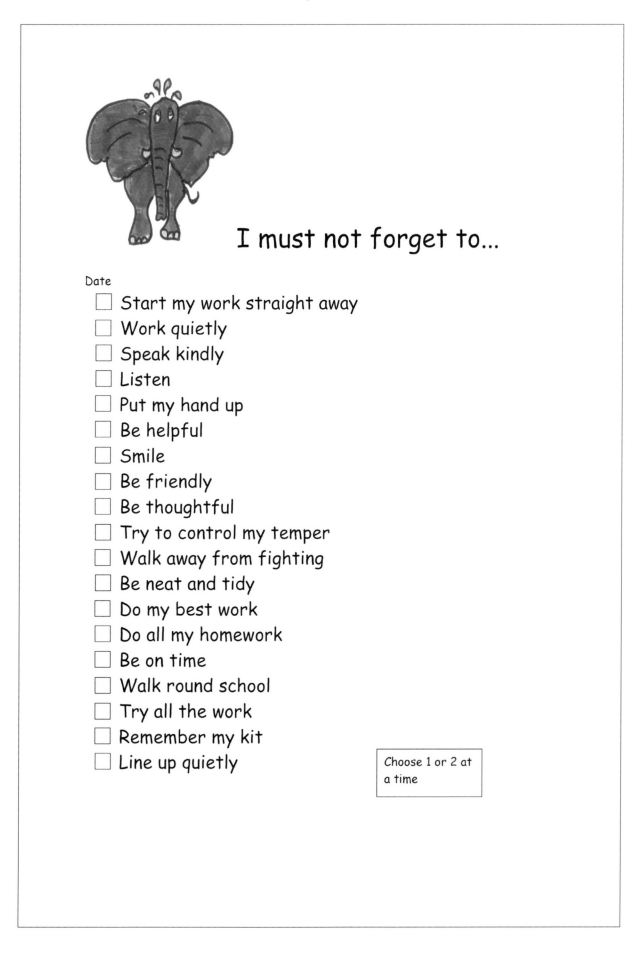

I must not forget to...

Date

- ☐ Start my work straight away
- ☐ Work quietly
- ☐ Speak kindly
- ☐ Listen
- ☐ Put my hand up
- ☐ Be helpful
- ☐ Smile
- ☐ Be friendly
- ☐ Be thoughtful
- ☐ Try to control my temper
- ☐ Walk away from fighting
- ☐ Be neat and tidy
- ☐ Do my best work
- ☐ Do all my homework
- ☐ Be on time
- ☐ Walk round school
- ☐ Try all the work
- ☐ Remember my kit
- ☐ Line up quietly

Choose 1 or 2 at a time

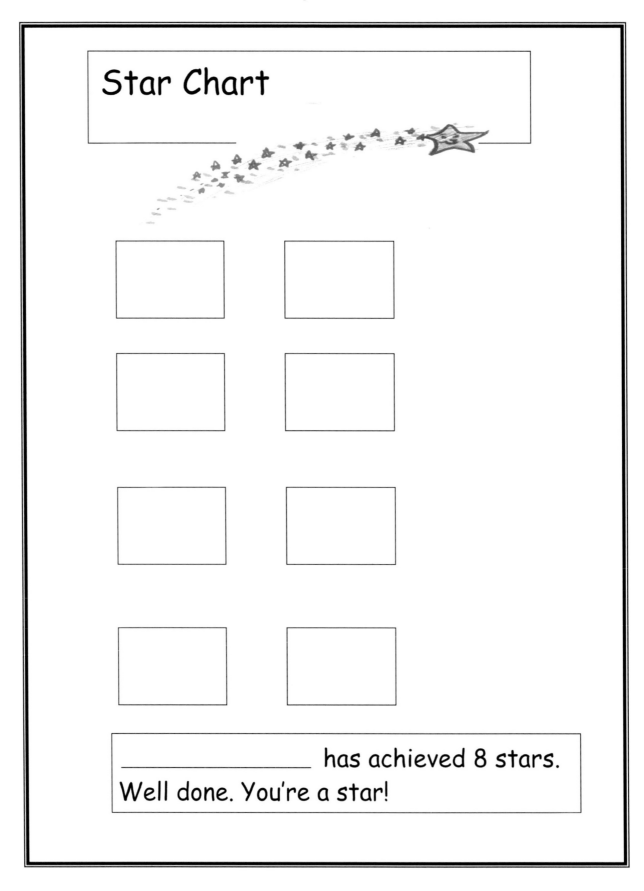

Star Chart

_____ has achieved 8 stars.
Well done. You're a star!

----

showed star quality when

Well done!

Signed ------------------------------- Date -------------------

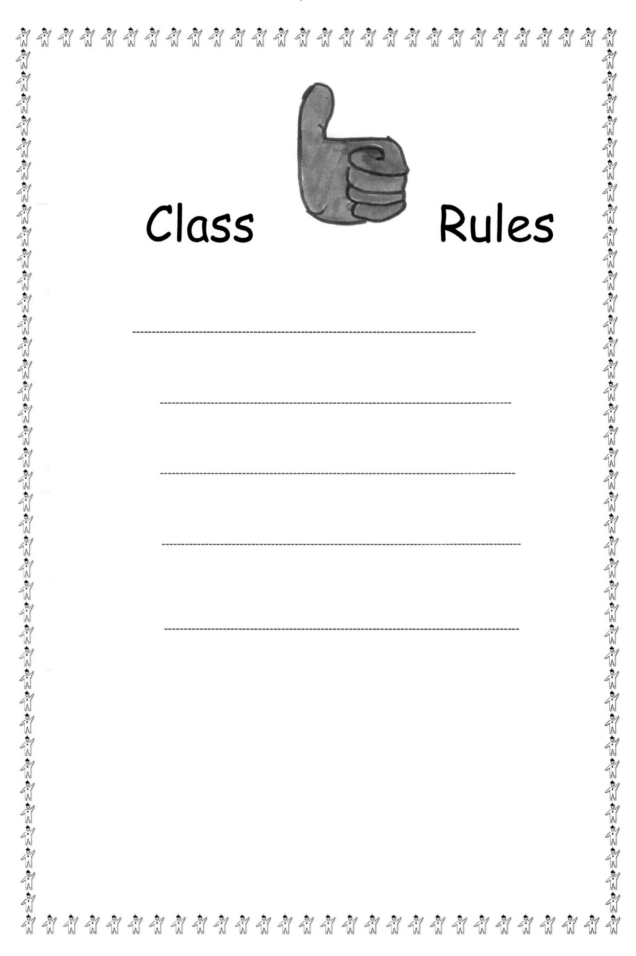

Class Rules

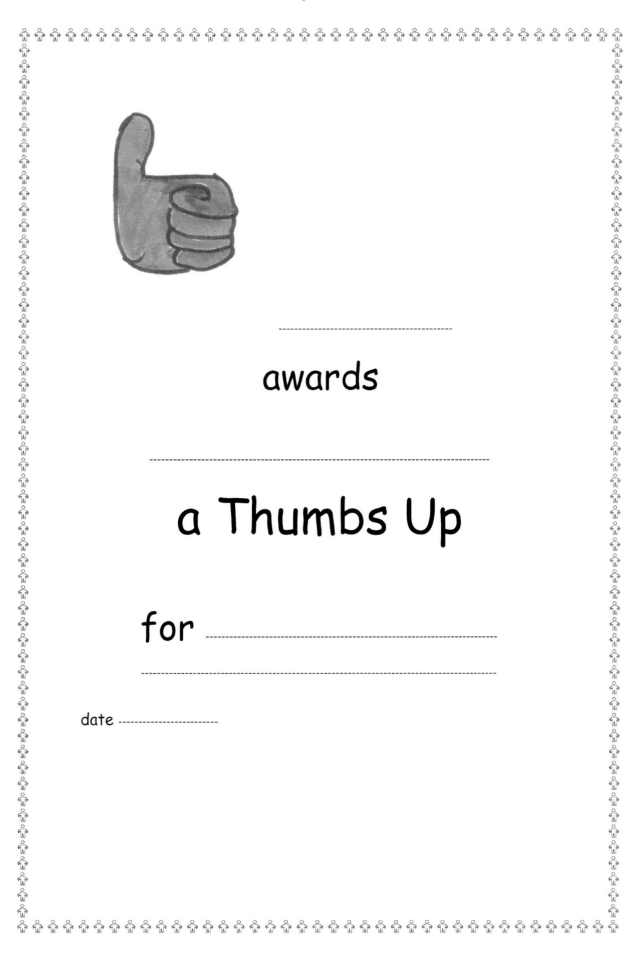

----

awards

----

a Thumbs Up

for _____

_____

date ----------------------

---

is a winner because

Keep it up!

Signed --------------------- Date ------------------

Suggestions for lunch/playtime activities

Some children will need more support than others to learn and carry out the rules. Games which can be organised by support assistants or lunchtime supervisors in order to promote better behaviour at lunchtimes include:

SKITTLES

A set of skittles (choose a good size that is easy to stand up) are useful for encouraging turn-taking and anticipation (empty lemonade bottles containing sand may be used); and Ready, Steady, Go!-type games.

PLASTIC GOLF SET

This is not necessarily a team game but something children can develop an interest in. Try to create distinct targets rather than allowing aimless hitting of the ball, e.g. large cardboard boxes on their sides with arch-shaped holes cut out are ideal.

TENTS, TUNNELS AND CUBES

Pop-up play tents, tunnels and cubes are readily available, easy to store and have great potential for games. Pop-up cubes can be used as easy targets for throwing balls and beanbags.

THE 'CHOSEN' ONE

A way to choose fairly who is the 'chosen' one. Children put their fists out. The rhyme goes round:

Dip, dip, dip, my blue ship
sailing on the water,
like a cup and saucer.
Dip, dip, dip, you are it!

The child whose fist it lands on is 'it'.

HOOPLA

Small hoops or hollow-disc frisbees are useful for hoopla games (use lemonade bottles filled with sand for targets).

WHAT TIME IS IT, MR/MRS WOLF?

One player stands out in front with his/her back to the rest of the players. The others creep up behind calling 'What time is it, Mr/Mrs Wolf?' The leader turns around calling a time and the other players must freeze. If the leader calls 'dinnertime' the pupils run back over the line and the one caught becomes the next 'wolf'.

ROLL THE BALL

Players sit in a circle. The players have to roll the ball out of the circle to score a point. The aim is to roll the ball out of the circle. This gains a point. The ball is fetched back by the scorer. Points may be scored individually or as teams.

'QUEENIE-O, QUEENIE-O'

A 'queen' is chosen who stands at the front facing away from the others. Queenie throws a small ball over his/her shoulder. One person gets the ball and hides it behind his/her back. Everyone else hides their hands behind their backs. The players call out 'Queenie-o, queenie-o, who's got the ball-io?' Queenie turns around and tries to guess. If correct, that child becomes queen.

NAME BALL

Players form a circle with one player in the centre. Players throw a ball in the air and call out the name of one of the other players. That player must try to catch the ball before it bounces more than once. If that player does this, he/she takes the place of the player in the middle.

TAG

A catcher wearing a band counts to 20. The catcher touches the pupils, who have to stand still. Keep going until everyone is caught. The last person to be caught is the new catcher, or the adult chooses.

DUCK, DUCK, GOOSE

Everyone sits in a circle. One person is 'on'. That child goes around the outside of the circle touching everyone on the head and saying 'duck'.

When the child taps someone and says 'goose', both run around the outside of the circle in opposite directions and try to get to the empty space first.

FRUITS

Children stand in a circle. They are alternatively given the fruits orange, banana, apple, strawberry, grapes. The caller calls a fruit and all children in that category leave their places and run around the outside of the circle in a clockwise direction. The first one back to his/her place calls the next fruit. While children are running around, the caller might also call fruit, and they then have to run in the opposite direction.

A narrative observation

Name:	Date:
Lesson:	Time:
Class teacher:	Observed by:

Issues arising from observation

Future strategies

An ABC observation

	Date:
Name:	
	Time:
Lesson:	
	Observed by:
Class teacher:	

Context of incident

Antecedent

Behaviour

Consequences

Additional comments

Issues arising from observation

Future strategies

An event-sampling observation

Name:	Date:

Lesson:

Time	Behaviour	Duration	Outcome

Issues arising from observation	Future strategies

A time-scaling behaviour observation

Name:	Date:

Lesson:

Time	Behaviour	Behaviour of randomly selected control pupil

Issues arising from observation	Future strategies

Example of a tracking observation sheet

Name ....   Date..

Weekly target...   Overall rating ....

Rating 1(poor) ————— 5 (excellent) please circle

Monday	Tuesday	Wednesday	Thursday	Friday
Subject: Teacher:	Subject: Teacher:	Subject: Teacher:	Subject: Teacher:	Subject: Teacher:
Rating 1 2 3 4 5 Comments	Rating 1 2 3 4 5 Comments	Rating 1 2 3 4 5 Comments	Rating 1 2 3 4 5 Comments	Rating 1 2 3 4 5 Comments
Break				
Subject: Teacher:	Subject: Teacher:	Subject: Teacher:	Subject: Teacher:	Subject: Teacher:
Rating 1 2 3 4 5 Comments	Rating 1 2 3 4 5 Comments	Rating 1 2 3 4 5 Comments	Rating 1 2 3 4 5 Comments	Rating 1 2 3 4 5 Comments
Lunch				
Subject: Teacher:	Subject: Teacher:	Subject: Teacher:	Subject: Teacher:	Subject: Teacher:
Rating 1 2 3 4 5 Comments	Rating 1 2 3 4 5 Comments	Rating 1 2 3 4 5 Comments	Rating 1 2 3 4 5 Comments	Rating 1 2 3 4 5 Comments
Subject: Teacher:	Subject: Teacher:	Subject: Teacher:	Subject: Teacher:	Subject: Teacher:
Rating 1 2 3 4 5 Comments	Rating 1 2 3 4 5 Comments	Rating 1 2 3 4 5 Comments	Rating 1 2 3 4 5 Comments	Rating 1 2 3 4 5 Comments